The Unfulfilled Promise

The Unfulfilled Promise

Sonia Thompson

Copyright © 2024 by Sonia Thompson.

All rights reserved. No part of this book may be reproduced in any form or by any electronic or mechanical means, including information storage and retrieval systems, without permission in writing from the author and publisher, except by reviewers, who may quote brief passages in a review.

ISBN: 979-8-9909505-5-9 (Paperback Edition)
ISBN: 979-8-9909505-6-6 (Hardcover Edition)
ISBN: 979-8-9909505-4-2 (E-book Edition)

Book Ordering Information

Executive Book Agency, US
1968 S. Coast Highway
#4214 Laguna Beach, CA 92651
Phone Number: +1 (949) 415-3402
Email: admin@executivebookagency.com
www.executivebookagency.com

Printed in the United States of America

Contents

Introduction vii
Synopsis xi
Prologue xiii

2003 1
2004 9
2005 26
2006 54
2007 84
2008 138

Afterwards 167

Introduction

In October 2002, I attended a seminar in radio. I was not the typical student on this course. I say this because I am a totally blind person, whose parents came from Jamaica. My mother ran her own grocery shop and my father worked as a carpenter. I am the fourth child of a family of eight, and I am the only one who is disabled. My oldest brother, Ronald, was not born in England like the rest of us.

*

I arrived in this world six weeks early and I had a hole in my heart and congenital cataracts. This meant that I spent a lot of time in the first years of my life going to and from hospitals. I can recall staying in hospital for my eyes, but not for my heart.

During one of the operations I had on my eyes, I lost the sight completely in my right eye and was left with a little bit of vision in my left. However, this does not appear to have caused me any problems Until I went to junior school.

One of the teachers who taught me noticed I was not managing as well as the other children in my class, so I left and went to a school for children with partial sight.

The school I went to was relatively new and it was further away from home. The local education authority arranged for a taxi driver to take me there in the mornings, and for one to pick me up in the afternoons. One of the things that was unusual about this school was that the girls were taught how to sew.

In the hall, which served as a dining room, a stage and a gym, the sewing teacher would set out long tables, along which we would spread ourselves out. Under her tutelage, I made two dresses, two skirts, a blouse and a couple of bags. Sewing hems was the only aspect of dressmaking that I found difficult. This was because I did not have enough sight to do that fine work. When the hall was used as a dining room, the dinner ladies laid out tables which were octagonal in shape, at which we ate our lunch.

A member of staff sat with us at these tables, and he or she shared the food we would eat. The meals ranged from steamed fish and chips (with a warning to mind the bones), stew and dumplings and ham and parsley sauce. The puddings consisted of spotted dick, blancmange and semolina. Another thing that was different about this school was the way a few of the lessons were delivered.

Some of them came from a speaker on the wall. While many of these lessons just required us to sit and listen, others expected us to get involved by singing along to the folk songs and doing physical activities. The other thing I liked about this school was the holidays.

Every year, the school arranged for a group of us to go to Bognor Regis in Sussex for a fortnight. We always stayed in a large house, which was by the seaside. During our sojourn, we visited places of historical interest such as The Victory in Portsmouth, Arundel castle, and Chichester cathedral. I went for three years running. After my last visit, I won a prize for the diary that I had written. It was obvious the headmaster did not think a girl would win because the award I received was *Caverns of the Moon* by Patrick Moore. When the time came for us to go to Bognor Regis the following year, I decided not to go. I had had another operation on my eyes, which turned out not to be successful. The headmaster, who was the only member of staff I liked at this school, was very disappointed. Not long after I had started to go to this school, we left the house we were living in.

We moved into a three-bedroomed house, which my parents could afford without any help from anybody else. At the time when we took up occupancy, the house did not have a bathroom, so my father got one built later on. What was significant about this change of address was that we moved into a house opposite a church.

One of my earliest memories of life in this house was the arrival of my youngest sister, Frances. I wanted my parents to call her Marilyn, but they had other ideas. After her christening, a lot of guests came back to the house, many of whom I never saw again. In time, a new vicar was installed, and he played a huge role in our lives.

On a Sunday, we went to the morning service, Sunday school and to evensong. This vicar confirmed my mother and my second eldest brother, Gregory. Eventually, we joined the choir. My third eldest brother, Winston, became the boat boy, swinging the incense each Sunday morning. The vicar was a generous host.

On bonfire night, he invited us to attend the firework display he put on in the vicarage garden. As we watched a neighbour set off fireworks, we tucked into our mugs of soup and jaket potatoes. The vicar provided other entertainment in the vicarage.

One year, he asked us to join him for Halloween. Once we were all comfortably settled, he started to read a ghost story, but this was spoiled by one of the lads saying that he had seen a movement by the curtains. We played our part in other activities related to the church.

We helped out at jumble sales and at Christmas Bazaars. The vicar even co-opted us to take part in a play. When we weren't at school or church, we amused ourselves by playing in our little garden.

We played hopscotch, shops (using cereal boxes as bags) and we made a go-cart on which we rode around the block. But one of the things I liked doing most was watching the television.

I watched many of the children's programmes, the wrestling, the sports report and some of the dramas such as *Dixon of Dock Green,* and the Saturday evening entertainment. But all of this came to an end when my father announced that we were moving.

*

Although I have given an account as to how this period in my life began, according to an acquaintance it started like this: the author who ran the seminar in radio, told BNUK about my existence.

I joined this course because I had discovered there was much more to radio than radio one. As a consequence, radio became my companion.

Synopsis

After hearing items on the radio that reminded me of stories that I had written, I had a psychic experience in which I was led to believe if I made contact with the station concerned, somebody would get In touch with me. I made the contact, but nobody answered my communications.

As a consequence, I got involved with radio. Everything was going well until I tried to get on to postgraduate courses in broadcast journalism.

According to a clairvoyant who I contacted, I was being "prevented from getting onto the courses," and in a premonition that I had, I was warned that a journalist, "was dealing with my applications."

Meanwhile, family and friends were asked to record what I was doing. These recordings were converted into a package which, when broadcast, would force me to respond. My sister implied that it was all about work but when a vacancy came up and I applied for it, I did not get the job.

Prologue

BNUK (Broadcasting Network for the United Kingdom) gave me permission to write a letter of complaint. My grievance spanned a period of five years and the letter was ten pages in length. By return of post, I received a two-page letter denying everything that I had alleged. For a moment, I thought I was mad, but when I thought about it, I realised they could not admit to anything that I had claimed. This was because what they tried to do - and they were trying to do something - had not worked.

Others closely involved in this fiasco have sought to distance themselves from it - some to the extent they want to believe that it never happened. I wish I could believe that it didn't happen too, but I can't because it was about my life.

Do you believe in psychic senses? If somebody had asked me this question five years ago, I would not have known what to say.

Now, I do know what I would say.

According to Sally Anne from the Psychic Line, "Anyone who discovers that you have a psychic sense will play around with it like a toy. Under no circumstances should you allow that to happen."

James Van Praagh says that people who prey on people who have psychic senses are what we call "psychic vampires."

2003

February 2003

Not a lot to record today, except I heard an item on *The Change*, which had a familiar ring about it.

On the programme, the presenter and guests were talking about friendships between women. According to what they were saying, when a woman makes friends with another woman, it is for life. This reminded me of the story that I had written.

My story was about two women who had fallen out. It was based on a real experience. I dismissed the matter as a coincidence. There was no way that anybody from BNUK could have seen what I had written. The only person who knew about my story was the tutor who had marked it.

For the past year, I have been a member of a book club. This month, we discussed *The English Passengers* by Matthew Neale. I liked the novel, and so did the rest of the group.

May 2003

I heard a second piece on *The Change* which made me think about another one of my stories.

Earlier in the year, I had written a short story about a single mother who was raising her child on her own without any financial help from her partner.

On the programme, the presenter and guests were talking about single motherhood, and one of the women taking part was Heather Small from M People. Heather Small may have been a single mum, but she was hardly on the breadline. Again, I disregarded the matter as a concurrence. Nobody could have seen what I had written.

In the book club, we discussed Angela's Ashes by Frank McCourt. I liked the memoir, but for some members of the group it brought back bad memories.

June 2003

I realised something. It was possible for BNUK to have got hold of my work. At the time when I heard the ideas that I had written about being debated on *The Change,* I was doing a creative writing course on a correspondence basis. The course material came in the form of printed booklets. I'm a registered blind person, so I had to get this material transcribed into a medium I could access. The organisation which could do this was the Royal Association for the Blind (RAB). RAB is one of the sources for BNUK's programme about people with sight problems, *Excuse Me Please*. Struck by this realization, another more powerful idea came into my mind: you must get in touch, and somebody will contact you.

It was a persistent concept, and for a while, I didn't know what to do. It was clear (or so it seemed) that if I got in touch, somebody would contact me. The other thing was, I had to make this communication via a phone-in. I cast around for a phone-in to get on to, but they all seemed to be talking about subjects that required experience in a particular area.

July 2003

Today, I heard about a phone-in that I could take part in. It was on a programme broadcast in the evening on my local radio station. I got on, but for the life of me, I cannot recall the subject I discussed. The following evening, at around six o'clock, the telephone rang. As soon as I put my hand on the receiver, it stopped ringing. *Who was it? Was it the person who was supposed to contact me?* I would never know, so I dismissed the matter as madness and thought no more about it until a fortnight later, when BNUK ran a week of programmes about forthcoming legislation relating to access for disabled people.

When I heard the trailer for this programme, I felt sure I would take part in one of the conversations, but events prevented me from doing so. On Monday, just before the show was about to begin, somebody tapped on my living room window. It turned out to be one of my brothers, Ronald, who was unemployed at that time.

I could not ask him to be quiet while the programme was being broadcast. He had come to see me, not to listen to a radio show. On Tuesday, an uncle who I had not seen for a long time visited me. He too came to chat, not to listen to the radio. On the day after that, I had arranged to see my niece, Abigail. She had said, "I'll come at ten o'clock in the morning," but at a quarter past ten, she rang to say, "I'll be late." She arrived just as the programme was due to begin. After Thursday's show, I felt I ought to make a contribution.

At that time, I wasn't online. I wrote down what I wanted to say that evening. The following day, after I had done my shopping, I went to the library and asked the person on duty if he could help me. It wasn't the sort of thing librarians should do, but I had to ask. Fortunately, the person I spoke to was able to grant my wish. Using his own email address, he sent my note. As I lay in my bed some hours later, I wondered what I had done. I experienced the most excruciating ear-burning sensation ever.

Superstitious lore says that if your ears are burning, somebody is talking about you. If your hands itch, you are going to either receive or lose money. If, however, your feet itch, you are going to travel. I had experienced these sensations quite a lot over the past few months and could not understand what they were attributable to. I had made no arrangements to travel, and I had not applied for any jobs. Therefore, were these sensations meaningful? The question you might be asking is this: why should BNUK be interested in me?

In 2001, a careers adviser had suggested that I should contact BNUK about doing a work experience placement. She gave me all the information I needed, and I left her office with every intention of getting in touch. At that time, BNUK used an answering service for the recruitment of staff on to its work experience programmes. The system asked questions and the person making contact had to respond to them. I was in the process of answering these questions when one came up about age.

Six years earlier, in 1995, a careers adviser had encouraged me to contact BNUK with regard to doing a work experience placement. I did so, and was rejected on the grounds that I did not have any experience and that I was too old. Six years later, the system was asking me how old I was. If I was too old in 1995, I was ancient in 2001. I replaced the receiver. I saw no point in going ahead with the call. This left me feeling depressed. However, I did not let this episode put me off.

At the same time, BNUK was running an employment scheme for disabled people. I decided to apply for a job on it. I reasoned, if I was turned down, it wouldn't be because of my age. I could cope with any excuse, except for hearing that I was too old. The scheme required that applicants apply for two vacancies. I did, and got neither of them. I wasn't successful because I lacked experience. Ultimately, I went off to Winstow University, where I studied and passed an introductory course in journalism. While on this course, I received an invitation to attend a workshop for the civil service.

I had forgotten that I had filled in a form for the civil service. Therefore, when I received a letter inviting me to attend a workshop, it came as a complete and utter surprise to me. I didn't really want to go, but my reader pointed out that I would have nothing to lose.

I went but arrived late. This was unusual for me. I'm one of those people who turn up in plenty of time. As soon as I sat down, a young man came up to me and asked, "Would you like to speak to the media?" I said no because I didn't know they were here. Later on, I realised that the presenter of *Excuse Me Please* was in attendance. The day should have been exciting, but I wasn't in the mood for it. That being the case, why on earth did I go ahead and apply for a place on the fast-track scheme? I don't know why I applied, but I didn't get a place. Perhaps, knowing of my failure, BNUK wanted to help me, but judging by what happened, was I really being supported?

Many years ago, I had found it necessary to consult a counsellor. Now, I turned to him again. I explained what I had experienced. He advised me to write a letter. At the time, I thought about doing so, but I changed my mind.

Who would I write to? And what would I say?

August 2003

I decided to write this note. I justified doing so on the grounds that there might be an opportunity I was missing out on. I will confess that the letter I wrote was vague and unclear. I addressed it to Donald Child, the presenter of Excuse Me Please. In it, I asked if he was targeting me and if he could let me have any information about courses run by BNUK. I received no reply.

September 2003

One day, the presenter of *The Customer*, mumbled a notice at the end of his show. It was an announcement to the effect that there would be more programmes on disability and benefit issues in the future. The promotion was so garbled that I asked my reader to check it on the internet. What I had heard was right.

In fact, the message prompted me to send in a comment about discrimination.

At this time, It occurred to me that there was no reason why I shouldn't try to get on to a phone-in in my own right, but before I could do this, a job club assistant drew my attention to an opportunity. Around about this time, I was looking for employment. A young woman called Kelly was helping me in my search. Kelly struck me as somebody who knew what she was talking about. One day, she told me about a vacancy at BNUK, in the central region. I couldn't believe it! It was on my doorstep. There wouldn't be any problems getting there. It sounded ideal.

October 2003

Two days before the closing date, I completed an application form, dictating the information to Kelly over the phone. We were sending the application online. It took a little bit longer than we had thought it would, but we got it done.

I was working on a radio play. It was much more difficult to write than I had thought it would be, but I liked the idea. Getting the balance right wouldn't be easy. The play was about a Christian woman who falls in love with a Muslim man.

In the book club, we read *Alias Grace* by Margaret Atwood. It went down well. We all liked it.

November 2003

I tried to get on to a phone-in about choosing the sex of your baby, but I couldn't get through. I thought about somebody I knew who had given birth to three boys and would have loved to have had a girl. On *Excuse Me Please,* the presenter was talking about disabled people having to use motorised buggies at airports and railway stations, whether they liked it or not. I sent in a comment pointing out that I would have missed my train had I not used one of these vehicles.

December 2003

I got onto a phone-in. It thrilled me so much that I did not correct the presenter when he mispronounced my name. I talked about how the building of a new supermarket had regenerated the area where I live. Before the supermarket had come, Sandbury was like a ghost town. The only shop to speak of in the area was Woolworths, which didn't have much in it. I had done it, and that was all that mattered. So far as I was concerned, it was the end of the affair. I believed somebody was trying to help me, but there was no evidence to support this idea. I could focus my attention on what?

I had submitted the radio play that I had written to Dramatique. So what could I do now? Think about Christmas?

As usual, I spent Christmas with my sister, Norma, and my brother-in-law, Larry, and their two children, Samantha and Adam, who live in the hills. It was an uneventful Christmas.

On Christmas day, the children woke early to open their presents. They had received heaps of them. As Samantha and Adam tore wrapping after wrapping away, they shrieked with delight at the gifts their parents, relatives, and friends had bought for them. By the time lunchtime arrived, they had no appetite. According to Norma, "They like gammon," but when it came to eating it, they would not. In fact, they left the table before the meal was over. When Larry suggested that we should go for a walk, they weren't keen. When he insisted on going for a stroll, they changed their minds. Once they were outside, Larry found it difficult to get them to come back in.

Throughout the trip, the children came across things that either amused or distracted them. When they weren't being amused or distracted, they were competing with each other in some way.

Eventually, we returned home where we resumed eating and drinking. Not long afterwards, I said my goodbyes.

2004

January 2004

A new year and a new hope - but what would the year bring?

It brought an experience I thought I would never have again. It was so powerful that I almost dropped the saucepan I was holding. A couple of hours after listening to *The Customer,* I had the most excruciating ear-burning sensation. It was so strong that I considered mentioning it to my doctor when I next saw her. After hesitating for a while, I sent in a comment to *The Customer* about obesity. I received no response, nor was it read out. In an attempt to resolve the matter once and for all, I did something I thought I would never do – I went on *Questions Please.*

Questions Please is first broadcast in the evening, and then it is repeated the following day. I was unable to hear the first broadcast, but when I heard the repeat, I knew I had to get on to the phone-in which followed. I wanted to talk about Maxine Carr, the girlfriend of the man who had killed two girls several months earlier. I keyed in the number, and before I knew it, somebody answered. I told her what I wanted to say. I never expected to hear from her again, but I did. When she called back, she asked, "Are you sure you want to go on?" I told her that I was. The next thing I knew, I was on air, giving my view about this woman. I found myself having to respond to an email that a listener had sent in. I couldn't believe it! Just as quickly as I had gone on air, I was off. Thank goodness for that!

Later, I regretted what I had done. I had made a fool of myself. I had allowed myself to be psychologically bullied. I vowed never to go on to a phone-in again. If I went on, it would be because it was what I wanted to do rather than because I thought I would gain something from doing so. What I had expected to happen did not. This made me even more furious.

A fortnight after this experience, I heard a comment to the effect that some people only phone-in if the incentive is right. I wasn't sure what the remark meant, but I understood it to mean that people only rang in if there was something in it for them. I decided to write a note. In it, I explained that I had been on a phone-in in December, but my name had been mispronounced. I held on to the note for a while before I posted it.

The lack of a response to my participation in a phone-in raised questions in my mind: had I got things wrong? Was somebody playing around with me? Or did the person who should have replied not have the authority to do so? Of one thing I was certain: if there was any meaning in the experience I'd suffered, then there should have been a response. How, otherwise, would I know whether somebody was helping me or not? Let's face it; this wasn't a situation they could announce on the radio. I had to do something, but what? It occurred to me that a careers officer might be able to assist me.

When I had completed the course at Winstow University, an acquaintance told me about a place where I could get help with regard to my interest in radio. Despite walking up and down the road where this aid could be obtained, my friend and I couldn't find the building concerned. My brother, Ronald, also investigated the claim that there was a station where I could be supported, but he couldn't find it either. It was with this place in mind that I went to see a careers officer. I was sure she would be able to tell me where this station was.

February 2004

When I saw the careers officer (on the day that I eventually posted the note to BNUK), she had no idea what I was talking about. The only radio station in the area she knew about was only interested in people under the age of twenty-five. Nevertheless, she made inquiries about other stations and was put in contact with one at Westhampton. She spoke to the people at this station, and they agreed to see me. On the day I went to Westhampton, BNUK would have received my note.

That night, I had a very vivid dream in which I was leaving. I was saying goodbye to everybody I knew.

I had only ever visited Westhampton once before. One Saturday, my sisters and I had gone there to do some shopping. It was busy, and somebody kicked me on my shins. Nobody seemed to be looking where they were going, but that was a long time ago, and we were strangers to the town. Now, I faced the prospect of having to get to Westhampton on my own.

The people at the radio station told me what to look out for by way of a landmark. I recollected it as well as I could. However, when I was on the train, it crossed my mind that it would be easier if I got a taxi to the station. It was my first visit to the area, and I had no idea about the layout of the bus station. It transpired that getting a taxi didn't make things any easier.

The taxi driver had no notion of where the radio station was. When he gained an idea of which direction to go in, he took me as near to the radio station as he possibly could. Even so, he had to ask where the entrance was. When he found it, he left me on the doorstep, and I waited for somebody to let me in.

The door opened, and a woman called Carol introduced herself. She admitted me, and told Matthew that I had arrived. After a short while, Matthew came to greet me. He seemed pleasant enough. He led me into a room where there were two other people, Paul and Robert. I liked Robert straight away, and we got talking. I did not imagine, at this stage, that Robert would be so considerate towards me later on. Matthew helped me to fill in a form, and he decided he would teach me on my own. I could go in next week if I wanted. In other words, I had got a place. I couldn't believe it!

I ordered a taxi to take me back to the railway station and realised that I would have to find out about the bus station. Getting taxis is all right for one-off journeys but for regular ones...

It took me a long time to find my way around Westhampton bus station. Week after week, I arrived there and some kind soul always offered to help me to locate the stand I wanted. More often than not, the person with me had no idea about the layout of the bus station, so we wandered around like nomadic souls. Eventually, we would find stand S. The member of the public accompanying me would invariably enjoin whoever was at the bus stop to, "put her on her bus when it comes." Then he or she would depart. I learned the bus route itself much more quickly.

Any difficulties I may have had in the beginning, stemmed from the fact that Carol had advised me to ask for the arts centre. This confused some of the drivers. They did not know there was an arts centre on the road I wanted to get off on. One day, a driver understood what I meant, "You mean the college?" I supposed that I did. After this, I had no more problems. Travel Line had said that it would take ten minutes to get to the stop I wanted. At first, I timed the journey, and at a minute before the bus was due to stop, I asked the driver to let me know when I should get off. By doing this, I learned where to alight independently. Fortunately, the stop I got off at was outside the college. All I had to do was to walk back a few metres, cross over a road, and I was at my destination.

On entering the college, I would go to a receptionist who rang the station, and somebody would collect me. When I discovered where the studio door was, I went to it and let Matthew know I was there by ringing him on my mobile phone. Once I was inside, Robert always welcomed me warmly. He constantly offered to buy coffee and crisps, if I wanted them. Having obtained everything I needed, he would leave me in a room to wait for Matthew. When the time came, Matthew escorted me to the studio.

I spent my first week at WCR trying to sort out the computer. There were some lessons on a CD that Matthew wanted me to listen to, but we couldn't get the computer to work. He called the technicians to see if they could sort out the problem, but they couldn't. Matthew said, "You ought to go home until we've solved the predicament." When I went back the following week, I used the computer to read some of the lessons, but it wasn't set up in the way I liked. After a couple of weeks of working at the computer, I grasped the concepts Matthew wanted me to know, and he eventually introduced me to a broadcasting studio.

March 2004

Studio A was large, and so was the broadcasting desk that was in it. It reminded me of a ship - long and deep.

In this studio, Matthew showed me how to operate a broadcasting desk. Every week, he went through the same routine of showing me which buttons to press, and then he would disappear. Several weeks later, I found out that he could listen in to the broadcast I was making. The discovery embarrassed me. The programme I presented, off air of course, consisted of music (using my own CDs), facts and figures, and humorous quotes, among other things.

Meanwhile, back at home, I learned that BNUK was looking for people to, "educate the public about living with a disability." I wondered whether I should volunteer. Ultimately, I made up my mind to leave my details. What harm could it do? I wasn't sure whether I would hear anything further, but at least I had offered. Someone did phone me, but I wasn't in. Who was it that had called?

After vowing never to go on to a phone-in again, I couldn't resist trying to get on to one about the National Health Service. I rang in, but my comment wasn't wanted. However, the following afternoon, somebody dialled my number, but just as I put my hand on the receiver, it stopped ringing. The last time I tried to get on to a phone-in, I had to ask myself if I was doing it for the right reason. Realising that I wasn't, I left the matter alone.

April 2004

Not long after this, I heard a comment, the idea behind which was to dominate the next four years of my life.

The remark went along these lines, "Some disabled people abuse their role as helper to other disabled people." At that time, this expression was just words. Later, however, I understood its significance.

The radio play that I had entered for the competition with Dramatique came back. I started to work on it again.

May 2004

On one of the most glorious days in May of this year, I experienced an unusual event. I was at the railway station, waiting for the train to Westhampton. I was in the middle of a conversation with Melvin, one of the staff from the station, when his voice was eclipsed by another, which was as clear as crystal, saying, "You're going to be blackmailed."

This voice stunned me. What did this mean? Was it connected to the business with BNUK? If it was, I had done what I was meant to do, and more besides. I had got in touch, but nobody contacted me. What was going on? I did not know. Nothing like this had ever happened to me before. Now, I understand what that experience was all about. It was a premonition.

Premonitions are warnings of things to come, and they kept on coming for the next four years.

At the station the train pulled in, and Melvin put me on it. Throughout the journey, I dwelled on the experience, but once I got to WCR, I put it out of my mind.

June 2004

On a Friday morning, I did my housework. I always rose early and started to work straight away. I began in the bathroom, cleaning the sink and the toilet. Then I would go downstairs and clean the washbasin and the lavatory down there. Afterwards, I mopped the bathroom and kitchen floors. Following a break, I did my weekly shopping.

Fortunately (or unfortunately as some might see it), I live near a supermarket. Once a week, I turned up clutching my shopping list only to find that I had to wait for somebody to take me round the store. This was despite the fact that the supermarket had allocated me a personal assistant, Barbara, who was an excellent helper. She told me about any offers that were on, introduced me to new products that she thought I might like, read the cooking instructions on packaging, read the "sell by" and "best by" dates, and advised me what to do if I wasn't happy with the service. And, as we got to know each other better, she would take me to my back gate.

The rucksack in which I carried my shopping was always full, along with another bag. On the odd occasion, I used a carrier bag as well. There were times when, after doing all of this, I was tired. Sometimes I would feel so exhausted that I catnapped while listening to the radio. Was this what I did one Friday when I should have been listening to the radio?

Friday afternoons was one of the times when I went to the gym. I was halfway through my time on the cross-trainer when I experienced one of the most excruciating ear-burning sensations ever. What did it mean? Was somebody trying to kill me? It certainly felt like it.

On the following Monday, as I prepared my lunch, I heard a discussion on the radio that reminded me of the topic I had talked about when I had attended the Civil Service Board a couple of years ago – the National Health Service. How would they have found out what I had said? Surely, I was jumping to the wrong conclusion. Interviews, and what happens in them, are supposed to be confidential. Undoubtedly, that privacy would be respected, but had it been?

One of the women in the book club, Tracy, was friendly with a woman who worked at BNUK. Through comments I overheard her make to another member of the group, I realised that the conversation I had heard on the radio was no mistake. The premonition was right. This was an attempt at blackmail. What could I do about it? Who could I tell? I understood there was no alternative other than to let the matter drop.

Not long after this, I heard an item which struck me as a threat.

The presenter of *Excuse Me Please* suggested that, as BNUK only employed a few disabled people, it would be difficult to get into the organisation. In other words, it would not be easy to get into BNUK without The Child's (Donald Child's) help. Dangerous talk from somebody who had done nothing when I had contacted him. There's only one God. Anyone setting himself up as another is only going to cause trouble trying to prove as much. To believe you are the only person who can help means that you will have to do things you might not have intended to do, in order to prove your point.

A couple of weeks later I heard an item about shopping, so I submitted what I thought was a very good piece. It wasn't used. I sent in another comment about disabilities, but this wasn't read out either. No matter what I did, I never received a reply. I remembered that I was a listener, and listeners would not normally expect to receive responses to their communications.

July 2004

For three of the four weeks in July, I did not go to WCR.
According to the message I received, Matthew was ill.

Towards the end of the month, I heard a most peculiar thing on *Excuse Me Please*. The presenter was having some kind of a fit. At the end of the programme, he outlined the degree of disability his team had: he was blind; his producer was partially sighted, and so on. I heard a comment to the effect that some disabled people didn't want to be helped by other disabled people. Evidently, the presenter had found out that WCR was supporting me. From time to time, Matthew had to work for BNUK.

How ironic. Earlier in the year, The Child had alleged that some disabled people abuse their role as helper to other disabled people. How pathetic! Did he say this because of me? I thought he did, and set about writing a note. I phoned Matthew to see if he could give me a hand with the delivery of an email. He said, "Of course, I will." I had every intention of dispatching a note, but as soon as I arrived at WCR, I changed my mind. The last thing I wanted was to become embroiled in a slanging match. Transmitting this sort of email would go against me. Instead, I discussed the matter with a professional.

August 2004

Once upon a time, registered blind people had a social worker they could call on if they needed any help. The woman who I could contact if I was experiencing any difficulties used to be a teacher, but somehow she had got involved with social work. Her name was Louise Heart, and I phoned her and she agreed to see me. She listened to what my problem was, and when I had finished telling her my tale, she asked me one question, "Has anyone ever responded to any of the comments that you've sent in?"

"No," I told her.

"Leave this matter alone," she said. "It's all coming from you."

She pointed out that there are millions of people who listen to the radio. I knew this. Once again, she advised me to abandon the affair and to get on with the play I was writing.

How wrong she was. It wasn't all coming from me. When she left, I thought through what she had said. Louise had come to the same conclusion as I had done: if there was anything in the situation, somebody should have got in touch with me. There are millions of radio listeners, and contacting me would be the only way of letting me know whether someone was going to help me or not.

In the end, Louise left me feeling vulnerable, deceived, and cheated. Perhaps, because I felt that she wasn't entirely right, I turned more and more to clairvoyancy. I really believed the experience was meaningful, but in the absence of any response, I had to think again or eventually face up to the fact that there was something wrong with me. On the other hand, if I was right, I was in contact with a psychic vampire. A psychic vampire is somebody who, having discovered that a person has a psychic ability will do nothing but prey on it. For three years, I kept my mouth shut about this affair.

In the meantime, I hatched a plan. I decided I would continue to send in comments and notes until I submitted the play I was working on. Once I had done that, I would have nothing more to do with this business.

September 2004

An item came on *The Customer* about a teacher who had taken the school he taught at to the Disability Rights Commission. In fact, the teacher had won his case. On hearing this, it never occurred to me that The Child was trying to blackmail me over a teaching experience that I'd gone through.

In September 1995, I had taken up my place on a teaching course for further, adult and higher education at Lowtown University. In order to do this course, it was necessary for me to move away from home. This being the case, I knew that I would have to sort out any help that I would inevitably need, such as mobility.

I needed somebody who could show me the layout of the college campus and of the town itself. I organised the orientation I needed and knew it was there whenever I wanted it. Within twenty-four hours of arriving at the college, a mobility officer showed me the campus, and later that week, the same person introduced me to the town.

The university told me, "You will do your first teaching practice at the nearby college." This was easy to get to, but difficult to get back from. Nonetheless, I managed. When, however, the time came to do the next block of teaching practice, nobody sought a placement for me. I complained, and I found that while Simon Richards, one of the lecturers, was keen for me to have a teaching practice, Kenneth Wilkes, the principal lecturer, was not. Kenneth Wilkes did his best to make sure I didn't have a placement to go to. I aired my grievances more and more, and eventually, Simon Richards found a teaching practice for me.

This involved going into another town, which turned out to be quite good. It was a positive teaching experience, and my only regret was that I wasn't there for longer. As a result of this success, Kenneth Wilkes undertook to find me a placement. The only problem was, it clashed with one that Simon Richards arranged at the university itself. Because I was unable to take up the placement that Wilkes found, he accused me of not wanting to teach. More arguments followed, but the situation was finally resolved when the institute awarded me a pass for the teaching I carried out, and gave me a certificate. Despite receiving the certificate, when the time had come, I could not wait to leave.

Although there was only three of us at the book club - Tracy, Michael, and myself - they discussed me as though I wasn't there. It was clear they were alluding to the piece which had been broadcast on the radio. As a consequence of this exposure, that meeting of the book club was very tense.

Tracy wasn't a particular fan of mine, and I wasn't a supporter of hers. Throughout the meeting, she did nothing but try to belittle everything I had to say about the book we were discussing. *The Unbearable Lightness of Being* by Milan Kundera wasn't the easiest of books to read, but to have had everything I had tried to say derogated, was hurtful. That particular meeting ended early, and my spirits rose when I left.

The Unfulfilled Promise

Undermining, ruining - call it what you will - was definitely in the air. I had no doubt in my mind that The Child was out to destroy me. He presented a programme in which a piece appeared about wrecking people's reputations. Gerald Ratner was named. If my memory serves me right, he ruined himself by making disparaging comments about the jewellery his chain of shops sold.

Believing that this comment was aimed at me, once again, I wrote a note. Before I knew it, I was at the library asking for help to send an email. On this occasion, nobody could assist me. A wave of relief passed over me. The sort of comment I was intending to make would not have got me anywhere. I saw myself as being above this level of behaviour. Grateful that a librarian could not help me, I returned home. When the presenter announced an item on bullying, I knew I would have to say something.

In the meantime, at WCR, a change was about to take place. For some reason that I cannot recall, I phoned the station. I was probably ringing to check if it would be all right to go in on the following day. Paul answered the phone, and we got talking. "Matthew isn't supporting you in the way he should be," he said. "Matthew should have stayed in the studio with you and taken you through various processes." I wasn't surprised to hear this.

Long ago, I concluded that, although Matthew had taken me on, he had never expected to see me again. Therefore, this news did not shock me. But what could I do about this discovery? Who could I turn to for help?

The next time I went to WCR, Matthew wasn't there.

Nobody explained his absence to me. Rather than go home, I headed for the studio where I presented a jazz show. Looking back, I wonder how I had managed to do this - operate a broadcasting desk while having to read a Braille script.

When I went to WCR a week later, a development had taken place. As soon as I crossed the threshold, I saw Robert. He told me, "Matthew's no longer working at the station because he's fallen out with the management team. Apparently, he agreed to leave at Christmas, but in a showdown, he handed in his notice on the spot." I never found out the details of what had happened. All I learned was that Matthew had not been happy at WCR. But what did this mean for me? Where did I stand?

October 2004

My view on bullying is simple. It's despicable. Those who ill-treat others should be regarded in the same light as those who harass, assault, and cause actual bodily harm. The same level of hurt and distress is being meted out to someone. In fact, bullying is worse, because it's about humiliating someone. Despite sending in my opinion, I received no response. Perhaps this was because it wasn't a favourable comment.

Work on my play was coming to an end. Two weeks later, I submitted it to BNUK. I received a postcard saying, "It will take four months to process."

I was presenting my off-air show when Robert popped in to see me. He said, "I'll help you if you want." I accepted his kind offer, and during the following week, my training as a radio presenter began.

One of the things Robert taught me was how to tell an anecdote. I found myself talking about experiences that I'd long forgotten about. He was highly amused by some of them and perhaps an audience would have been too.

In August 1995, my sisters, Frances and Martha; my nephew, Patrick; and I had gone on a coach touring holiday in Italy. Our first stop was in Florence. When we got on the coach to go to our next destination, Rome, there was a bit of a commotion because a woman wanted to sit next to her son. Apparently, during the overnight journey they were separated. Max, the tour leader, made sure that mother and son were together, and we proceeded on our way to Rome. After Rome, we went to Assisi, and then we visited Venice. This was our last stop.

Once we'd eaten our breakfast and done anything else we needed to do, we made our way to the coach. When we got on to it, we found that the woman and her son were sitting in the very seat that Frances and I usually sat in. We were taken aback. A disturbance broke out. This was outrageous. Why, of all the seats on the coach, did she take ours? On these holidays, the custom is that a seat rotation takes place.

After each journey, passengers are supposed to move back a seat or two to enable everyone to get a chance to sit at the front. However, our tour leader did not put this rotation into practice. The woman concerned calculated that, if Max implemented the seat rotation, she would have been sitting in the seat that Frances and I normally occupied.

Max, the tour guide, came onto the coach and ordered everybody to get off. Then we got back on, and sat in the seat Max indicated. One woman, a black woman, loudly proclaimed that she wasn't moving for anyone, and she didn't either. She remained seated on the back seat. By the time we were all seated and the journey was underway, it occurred to me that it didn't really matter where we were sitting now because the holiday was over, and we were going home.

Robert taught me how to end these stories by giving them a punch line. I practised this technique by talking about a television programme that enthralled me. We also practised discussing topical subjects. Our exchange of views worked really well. Between us, we enjoyed ourselves. I will always remember his kindness.

November 2004

I wrote an article about bullying. When I had finished writing it, I asked the lecturer who had taught me at Winstow University if he would read it. He did, and made one or two comments on the piece. It was much better than I had thought it was. The question was: did this man pass it on to people at BNUK? I heard an awful lot of talk about bullying at this time. Ultimately, I changed my mind about using it. An experience that Frances and I had gone through in a car park gave me another idea.

Ten days ago, Frances and I went shopping. We were trying to park on the car park at a shopping centre. We found ourselves going round and round like a spinning top. This gave me an idea for an article. As soon as I could, I set to work on it.

Around about the same time, I also applied for another job with BNUK. According to the careers adviser who helped me to fill out the form, "You should have been given a job." But I never heard from them again.

December 2004

I dreamed that I saw a fire. I didn't know what it meant. The following day, when I came back from a trip into Birmingham, I discovered that BNUK had turned my play down. This rejection disappointed me no end. I had put so much effort into writing it. Apparently, BNUK weren't able to commission it.

If there was any meaning in the psychic experience that I had endured, this could have been an ideal way of communicating something. Nothing was said, so I regarded the matter as closed. But was it?

The Unfulfilled Promise

Meanwhile, at WCR, Robert and I were about to present the last programme of the year. A young woman arrived and agreed to take part in a discussion about children. It went very well. The show had been a fine one, and overall, the undertaking had been positive. Robert had made a huge difference. But all good things must come to an end.

Robert told me he was leaving, "I'm going to work for an independent radio station." I wished him well and knew that I would miss him very much. Where did this leave me?

Dear Robert. Once again, he came to my rescue. He said, "I'll help you when I've settled into my new job."

It was kind of him to offer, but would he have the time and the inclination? Only time would tell.

I wrote an article based on the experience that Frances and I had gone through when we tried to park at a nearby shopping centre. At the end of the year, when the Tsunami in Indonesia was still headline news, I sent it to a magazine called *The Lady*.

2005

January 2005

A new year and a new hope - but what would this year bring?

Surely, it couldn't be any worse than the last one.

All that effort - all that effort in writing the play had come to nothing. Worse still, there was nowhere else I could send it to. Never again would I write a radio play. Well, I had done it and it was time to look forward, not back. Indeed, I had something to look forward to - Robert, Robert who had said that he would help me. The plan was that I would have to wait until he had settled into his new job. Once he had accomplished this, he would contact me, and we would pick up from where we had left off.

The only problem was the waiting. I couldn't wait. I wouldn't say I'm an impatient person, but I wanted to be doing something. I longed to be doing something so badly that I phoned him. His response electrified me. He said, "I don't know who you are." Was it really possible to have forgotten somebody who you had taught over a period of ten weeks, only a few weeks ago? I slammed down the receiver because I had nothing to say.

A few minutes later, the telephone rang; it was Robert, apologising for not recognising me. He was doing his shopping when I called and this appeared to have made him forget who I was. Suddenly, he sounded like the Robert of yore - keen, enthusiastic, and so cheerful. He said, "I'll contact Gerry, and will get in touch with you within the week." Gerry was the person who organised the broadcasting output at WCR. I thanked Robert, feeling a lot better.

The week passed, but I didn't hear from Robert. I was about to give up when he phoned me. He said, "I've spoken to Gerry, and he wants you to do another demonstration tape." I was more than prepared to do this. He said, "I'll contact you again." But before this took place, I received a call from a very unexpected quarter.

The woman on the other end of the phone introduced herself as Fiona. She said, "I'm the new manager at WCR." This was news to me because no one had ever talked about a replacement for Matthew. When I thought about it, I realised that the college would have appointed somebody to take his place.

Fiona invited me to return to the station. "Somebody has been taken on who can help you," she informed me. I told her about Robert. She couldn't see what the problem was. There was no reason why I shouldn't work with this person until Robert was ready to take over. After hesitating, I agreed to meet this person who could support me. Before I met him, I went to see a tarot card reader.

I don't know what prompted me to visit Shaun. Perhaps it was because I felt insecure and unsure about what was happening to me. I thought I was doing the right thing in responding to what I believed was an offer of help. Now, I regarded what had happened as a schizophrenic voice. But was it? The aid that I thought would come as a result of that experience had not arrived. Not one of the comments I had sent in had been answered. I assumed I was doing the only thing that was left to me: helping myself. I must admit, I knew nothing about tarot cards. I had consulted Shaun once before. The reading had not been a fantastic one, but I saw no harm in visiting him again. Shaun worked in a room on an upper floor in an office block. It was not a big room, but it always smelled of joss sticks. In the room was a table. On it stood a tape recorder. There were also a couple of chairs in the room too. A woman was ever present. Was she his partner? I never asked.

Shaun always started a reading by testing the tape recorder. Clients could, if they wanted, have their reading recorded. Once Shaun was satisfied that the tape recorder was working, he began the reading. First, he laid out several packs of cards on the table, "Choose a pack from one to seven," he would say. When I had selected a pack, he shuffled the cards and spread them out. He would ask me to pick out seven cards from those laid out on the table. The first card I chose indicated that the judgement I had made was the right one and that my mind was sound. I thought this alluded to the fact that I had decided to leave the matter alone. I had achieved nothing in pursuing it, so why not leave it alone?

The next set of cards suggested that I would meet somebody who could be of help and that he was close at hand. I mentioned the person I was going to see the following day, but the clairvoyant didn't seem to think it would be him. Whoever the cards were referring to would transform my life. The reading seemed to signal that I would go to London.

It all sounded encouraging, but would any of it come true? It is important to remember that clairvoyancy is only for guidance. What one learns might come true, but on the other hand, it might not. Whatever the reading may be, don't depend on it. It's like a weather forecast: sometimes it's right, and at other times, it's wrong.

The Unfulfilled Promise

Why bother with it in that case? Because it might provide an insight or a way forward in a difficult situation.

I left Shaun's office feeling pleased that I had gone, and knowing that my decision to abandon the affair was right.

The ten-minute train journey to Westhampton was over. At the bus station, I found stand S without any difficulties. While the journey was straightforward and familiar, WCR was not. I always arrived at the station early. This meant I had to wait until Matthew was ready. In the meantime, he would put me in a small room with a chair and a table in it. More often than not, I would take my Walkman out and listen to the radio. On this occasion, I had to wait, not in the small room, but in the reception area. I sat on a spacious, comfortable sofa. I could hear music drifting out of one of the studios.

Something was missing. WCR didn't feel right. What was it? It was the warm and friendly greeting from Robert that was absent. He had invariably volunteered to get refreshments for me, but there was no one to offer such a welcome on this occasion.

Eventually, a young man appeared. He sounded pleasant enough. Once we had introduced ourselves to each other, we went into one of the studios.

In studio B, which was my favourite because it was a reasonable size, we didn't do much. My purpose in coming was just to meet John and to discuss what I was going to do. I told him about the training I had done and mentioned there had been talk about me doing my own live programme. We agreed to carry on from where I had left off. Both of us liked this plan. Fiona, who joined us halfway through our meeting, approved of the arrangement too. I left WCR feeling that an objective had been achieved and that I would be getting on with something again. As soon as I stepped into my house, the telephone started to ring.

It was Robert. He could not contain his fury. He wanted to know what I'd been doing at WCR, "Alan said he saw you there this afternoon," he complained.

Words failed me. I did not know that Robert could behave like this. I tried to explain what had happened, but he was having none of it. Reluctantly, I agreed to wait until he had settled into his new job. It was touching that he was so keen to help me. But were his motives entirely pure? Anyone would have thought that he would have been glad to get me off his hands, especially in his circumstances, but that wasn't the case. I had to take him at his word and trust him. Before he rang off, he said, "I'll speak to Gerry. Once I've done that, I'll contact you again."

After all that, no progress had been made. It was all right for Robert: he had his job to occupy his time, whereas time weighed heavily on me.

Fiona must have heard about the event because she phoned me again. It was clear she didn't agree with what Robert and I were planning to do. Fiona said, "I don't trust Robert." I told her that I would have to. Robert was as good as his word, because he got in touch once more. He said, "Gerry said you can do a two-hour show."

That was much more than I was expecting. I didn't know whether to be pleased or not. He said, "We'll do a programme next week. I'll book the studio and contact you again." But when he got in touch, he said, "I've forgotten to reserve a studio."

Even though I had received a reading at the beginning of the year, I didn't dwell on it. What would have been the point? With clairvoyancy, things don't manifest themselves in the way you think they will or in any time span that may have been indicated. I had no idea how the introduction that Shaun had talked about would present itself. But it did, and it came in the form of a letter.

One year ago, I had found out about a community radio station called Palace FM, which ran a six-month course in radio presenting. I applied for a place on the course, but they turned me down. I reapplied, and somebody at the station told me, "The station will have to carry out an assessment to see if you can handle the equipment in the studio." I never heard from them again.

Now, out of the blue, they wrote to me, saying, "We're not going to give you a place." Instead, they told me about an organisation which offered a similar course-the Dual Heritage Development Agency (DHDA). DHDA was in Hallam. It wasn't too far away. Immediately, I contacted the agency. The person I spoke to confirmed that DHDA did run a radio course and that it lasted for four months. Students who completed the course successfully could do a placement at BNUK Central. The course would start in April, and they would let me have the forms as soon as they were available. It sounded like the opportunity I wanted. For some reason, known only to myself, I did not tell Robert about this discovery. With hindsight, keeping the information to myself was a very good thing to have done.

Robert phoned me to say that everything had been arranged. I was going to do my first programme on the following Friday (4th February). The plan was that I would meet Robert at Westhampton railway station, and he would ring to check that I was on my way. I couldn't believe it! Things were moving at last! But what was I going to do for my first show? I couldn't do anecdotes for an hour.

An idea struck. I could feature an item on cosmetic surgery -old and new. I found other material and put it all together. Also, Robert had agreed to take part in a discussion slot. I didn't have to worry about music because it was all stored on the computer.

February 2005

Before I knew it, the day had come and I was making my way to the railway station. As planned, Robert phoned me while I was on the train. Once I was at Westhampton railway station, I had to wait for him to arrive. I didn't mind having to do this; I saw it as a necessity because I would not have been able to get into the studio without him. What I did not know how to handle was all the inquiries from other passengers.

The public does not like to see a blind person standing alone. Every week, as I waited for Robert, I would be bombarded with questions of concern:

"Are you alright?"

"Are you waiting for someone?"

"Do you need any help?" And so on.

As politely as I could, I assured these good people that I was fine, and that somebody was coming to collect me. In time, Robert would turn up and apologise for being late.

More often than not, we went straight to the radio station. Every week, we jumped into a taxi to get us there, and Robert insisted on paying the fare.

It felt strange to be back at WCR with Robert. It was ever a quiet place to go in to, but on a Friday evening, it seemed even more peaceful. All I could hear was music pumping out of one of the studios. It always sounded as though the music was coming from afar. We only ever saw anyone as we were leaving. After signing ourselves in, we headed for studio C. By now, most of the studios at WCR had been upgraded, and contained state-of-the-art equipment.

The Unfulfilled Promise

After Robert had set things up, we were off. My first programme was underway. It felt tremendous, and we cried with delight at the result, despite the fact that Robert had to do a bit of editing. How fortunate I was to have had Robert to do this for me. Perhaps, for the first time, I realised that he was a patient young man.

Once Robert had edited the programme, and he stored it where Gerry could find it for broadcasting purposes, we ordered a taxi and went back to the railway station - a process that would soon become habitual.

We arrived at the train station with plenty of time to spare, so we always went to the waiting room where we had coffee and a chat. This was Robert's time. He would tell me about what he was doing. His new job was as a news editor for an independent radio station. Also, he co-presented a music programme, *Unsigned,* for another independent radio station. The programme aimed to offer a platform to bands who were not signed up with a record company. I don't know whether groups were taken on as a consequence of appearing on the show, but I thought the idea was a good one. I listened to the programme once, but the music wasn't to my liking. It was rock, heavy metal - call it what you will - but it wasn't for me.

Robert and I were opposites in every sense of the word: he was white, I black; he was six foot three inches tall, I five foot one; he came from a professional background, whereas I did not. There was an eighteen- year difference between us. In spite of this, we got on well together, even though from time to time, there were tensions between us.

The routine we fell into involved buying soft drinks. By the time we arrived at WCR, the cafeteria was closed. Robert would pop to the shop to get us something to drink. I could not help but feel that I was taking advantage of his good nature. This was the last thing I wanted to do.

One week, I remembered to add the drinks to my shopping list - Lucozade for Robert and ginger beer for me. When we got to the studio, I pulled them out of my bag and put them on the desk. I sensed that Robert did not like this gesture. I explained that it wasn't fair that he paid the taxi fares and bought the drinks. He didn't say anything, yet there would come a time when he would complain about paying taxi fares. This always took the form of him saying, "I'm going to claim the money back." If, however, I offered to pay, he constantly refused to accept any money. On one level, it was very decent of him, but on another, it would have been nice to pay my way. During the course of this partnership, strange things would happen to us.

One week, we arrived at the station only to find that we couldn't get in. Robert busied himself with contacting security. The person on duty that night was very difficult to track down. Eventually, he got through to somebody who said, "I'll come and let you in."

Fortunately, it wasn't too cold that evening. A silence fell between us. Suddenly, and without preamble, Robert mentioned psychic senses. It occurred to me that he had never come across such an idea before. He seemed to be amused by it. I said nothing, but why should he be mentioning this now?

Who had he been talking to? One thing was clear: I couldn't tell him about the experience I had sustained. He wouldn't have understood it. But there was no need to say anything because the security person came.

When an application form arrived from DHDA, I could not hide my delight. I felt sure I would be moving on and saying goodbye to the people at WCR. I filled in the form and sent it off.

Without any warning whatsoever, I received another challenge.

March 2005

The opportunity that came my way was a writing one. At first, I wasn't sure if I wanted to take part in the scheme. These competitions are so competitive. Did I stand a chance of winning? After some reflection, I decided to take part because I believed it would enable me to feel more stable. The business of the last few years had left me feeling distinctly insecure. There were times when I wondered what I thought I was doing depending on a young man like Robert. I was ashamed, but there was little I could do about it. He wanted to help me and I needed to be assisted, so I let him do so. I was inspired. A brilliant idea had come into my mind. Putting aside my reservations, I started to write.

Once I began to write, I wished that I had started sooner. With each and every passing day, the play developed and grew. When the time came to go away for a weekend, I regretted the fact that I had allowed myself to be talked into going.

Earlier in the year, I had received a phone call from a chap called Dennis, who wanted me to go to a conference. I wasn't keen on the idea, and I told him so. When I explained what my grievance was, he said, "Things will be different this time." He led me to believe he would like to see me again. Reluctantly, I had agreed to go.

In 1995 or thereabouts, I had joined The Association for Visually Impaired Teachers and Students (AVITAS). As the name suggests, the people in the association were students and teachers who were either studying or working in mainstream education. The idea of the group was that it would offer support to teachers and students. Throughout the year, members of the association received bulletins containing articles about members' experiences and matters relating to education.

The organisation's flagship event was the annual conference. This was always held at a university. Universities were able to offer the sort of accommodation the association needed -sleeping quarters as near to a conference room and dining area as possible. For many of the delegates, this conference was a lifeline. It gave them the chance to make new friends, catch up with old ones, and to have a jolly good time in the process. I attended these conferences for many years, and then I ceased going because of the way some of the delegates treated me.

At one of the conferences I went to, a woman approached me and pronounced that I was maturely dressed. I wasn't sure what she meant by this, but I interpreted it as meaning that I was well-dressed. On that particular day, I was wearing a pink cardigan and a black wrap-over skirt with pleats at the back. How I loved that skirt because it was so handy. It would go with almost anything. I wore it until there came a day when one of my sisters said, "You should bin it." While it felt all right, it looked faded and shabby. My understanding of what Tina said was wrong, as I realised later on. Her words signalled the beginning of a war.

Tina could see. This gave her the ability to wield an awful lot of power over people without sight. She was able to control the way they thought. This was what Tina managed to do, and I wasn't aware of it until I was due to go to a committee meeting.

At the conferences, Sunday mornings were always given over to elections. We elected people to stand on various committees. Delegates nominated and selected me to join a committee that looked into matters relating to education. The association was a national organisation. As a consequence of this, meetings were held wherever we could find a venue. This meant either going to members' houses or looking for a public building we could use. For instance, I arranged for some of the gatherings we attended to be held in a pub in Birmingham. On another occasion, somebody reserved a room for us in one of the buildings belonging to Leeds City Council. More often than not, gatherings were held at other people's houses.

The chairperson of the committee that I was a member of lived in Hull, but it was arranged that we would assemble at Tina's house in Leeds. I was so unwelcomed at Tina's house that I wasn't told about the gathering until afterwards. At another time, a meeting was held in Hull. While the rest of the committee stayed at the chairperson's house, I was compelled to book into a B & B. Throughout that weekend, the chairperson's attitude towards me was frosty, while another committee member strove to undermine everything I said. However, I did not let her get away with it. As we were waiting for our trains to take us back to our destinations at the end of the weekend, I laid into this woman in a way I would not have thought I would have done.

A few days later, I received a phone call from the membership officer, Gary, who took it for granted that the story he heard was right. He asked me to apologise, but I refused to do so. This meant he would have to go back to the woman concerned, and find out what really happened. Not long after this, I received another call, during which Gary asked me to forget about the matter and told me that I should keep quiet about it. I did not broadcast it, but I certainly didn't keep it to myself either. It was experiences like this that made me hesitate over agreeing to go to this conference, and I was right to do so.

April 2005

After a train journey which had taken six hours because of engineering works, I arrived at the venue, only to be greeted cursorily by the person who had urged me to come. Why had he invited me if he didn't want to spend any time talking to me? This treatment hurt me, but there was little I could do about it. I couldn't go home, so I would have to stay and make the most of the situation.

In many respects, the conference was the same. Speakers spoke about concerns that weren't unfamiliar: raising the aspirations of disabled students in further education with a view to getting them to consider going on to higher education; the standards required for recording material for blind and partially sighted people; and how the organisation would be affected by changes taking place at RAB.

After eating a three-course meal, we adjourned to the bar, where I met up with delegates who I had not seen in a long while. They welcomed me, and I wasted no time in catching up with their news. One person surprised me by now being the proud owner of a guide dog.

After imbibing several glasses of wine, I went to my bedroom. I could not sleep. I turned the television on, only to be greeted by the news that the Pope, John Paul II, had died.

Robert certainly knew how to take my breath away. We were in the middle of recording a show when he made an observation. I was reading my Braille script when he commented on the fact that I was only using one hand to read it. This was something that I would not have thought Robert would have any knowledge about.

When I was thirteen, I had an operation which should have restored my sight, but it did not. Instead, I lost the little bit of vision that I had left. As a result of this, I went to a school for the blind. It was a boarding school, which was in the countryside. On arriving at the school, nobody seemed to be expecting me. Nobody was prepared to offer any help. Where learning Braille was concerned, it was the maths teacher who taught me.

After every lesson, I stayed behind for long enough for him to give me a booklet about Braille. The first pamphlet contained the letters, A to J. I took it away, studied it, and then I picked up the next handout in the series. In this way I learned Braille, but how to read it was left up to me. I did what I thought was right. Using the index finger on my right hand, I read Braille. Later, I learned that Braille could be read using both hands. Often, I had tried to read Braille in this way, but I always reverted to the one-handed method.

The question was this: who had Robert been talking to? An idea crossed my mind, but I said nothing. What I did notice was that we were working together on the basis that I was going to aim for a placement, but this was never referred to again. Why? As smashing a young guy as Robert was, he was prone to moodiness. When he was in a bad state of mind, I had to put up with his rudeness. I never understood what put him in these moods. Frequently, I wondered if it was my fault. Sometimes he explained his gloominess by saying, "I'm tired." Remembering the fuss he had created when John could have supported me, he could not blame me. Saying that you want to help, and doing so, are two very different things. I will give him his due - he always apologised whenever he was impudent to me.

Good news! The article that I had written was accepted. *The Lady* magazine changed the title of my piece from *Parking for the Disabled* to *Parking Strife*. I could not conceal my delight over this achievement.

May 2005

Time was running out. Before I knew it, I had to think about finishing the play. When I inquired about the number of people who had entered scripts, the competition administrator said, "One hundred and fifty." That did not bode well. Would I stand a chance? I submitted the play, realising that if I didn't win this time, I could use it again later on. I posted it on the very last day. Only time would tell if it was going to be successful.

I had not heard anything from DHDA. I phoned them, but they couldn't give me a start date for the course. This was odd. It was as though they weren't in control of things.

At WCR, the programme was going well, or was it? On the very day when my play would have been received by Dramatique, we arrived at the station to find that we couldn't get into the studio. Robert ranted. He couldn't understand why such an error had been made. We had been going in on a Friday for long enough for the staff to know that one of the studios should be left open. He tried to get in touch with security. Nobody was around. He made another attempt. Still, he couldn't contact anyone. When he tried for a third time, he got through, and the person he spoke to said, "I'm on my way."

While we waited, we sat on one of the spacious sofas in the reception area. I really didn't know what had got into Robert that evening because he did nothing but complain. First, he moaned about the studio being locked. "On the one hand, when you're in the broadcasting industry, you expect these sorts of thing to happen, while on the other hand, they should not happen at all." Then he grumbled about the programmes we were making. Somehow, what we were doing was only a hobby. I wondered what had brought this mood on. He had seemed happy with the progress we were making.

It occurred to me that Robert was under somebody's influence. Whose was it? Unbeknown to Robert, the person whose spell he was under was the very individual who should have contacted me. Instead of getting in touch with me, it would seem that this person had contacted Robert. This would explain why he no longer talked about doing a placement.

What then did Robert discuss with this individual? Evidently, he wasn't being encouraged to put it into my mind that I should get in touch with him. Surely, this would have been the most obvious thing to do. So, what were they up to? What had The Child led

Robert to believe? I would have to talk to him to explain the experience I had endured - but it wasn't going to be a pleasant task to perform. This was a situation that had to be thought about and handled with care. Already, Robert had shown that he had no idea about the psychic world. After giving the matter much thought, my mind was made up: I was going to tell him how I had got involved with radio.

June 2005

Robert turned up at Westhampton train station early. It was probably the only time he got there before I did. Prior to jumping into a taxi, he insisted that we should have a coffee in the waiting room. We ordered our drinks and crisps, and once we were comfortable, I tried to tell him my tale. It wasn't going to be easy, but what was going on didn't feel right. I started then stopped. I started and stopped again. Robert said, "I won't laugh." That was hardly a helpful comment to have made. I tried again. I realised one thing: Robert would not have mocked me, but I found that I couldn't tell him my story anyway. I had told it once before, and I will never forget the response I received. Robert would never have understood. After a short pause, I said, "I can't tell you. It will have to be left alone."

Robert, however, was not prepared to drop the matter. We were in the middle of recording a show when he made a comment about mediums. To be honest, I did not know how to respond. I let it go. Later, I realised that, although Robert didn't know anything about the psychic world at that time, he had taken the trouble to find out about it. This was why he was able to speak so bitterly in the end.

Time was moving on. To my surprise, I had still not heard from the Dual Heritage Development Agency, the agency which Palace Radio had told me about earlier in the year. Three months ago, I had completed an application form and sent it off.

Despite the fact that I had been phoning the agency on and off, nobody had got in touch with me about a start date. would it ever happen? I began to doubt it.

Meanwhile, an idea had come into my mind. Why don't I do a postgraduate course in broadcast journalism? I began to make inquiries. I felt sure I was doing the right thing. A careers officer drew my attention to two courses, and I contacted the universities concerned for information about what they had to offer.

We were in the waiting room, drinking coffee, when I mentioned my plan to do a broadcast journalism course to Robert. He made no comment. On reflection, he may have been thinking about other things than me. One thing was clear: we wouldn't have much time left together.

In accordance with my desire to do a broadcast journalism course, I decided to write a newspaper article. It would demonstrate my keenness to get on to a course.

I wanted to write a piece about young adults. My reader knew somebody who I could talk to. He worked in the field of social work. My reader helped me to make an appointment to speak to this person, and on a bright Monday evening, I set out to go to her house, because it was where the interview was going to take place. The meeting went well. The social worker had so much to say both from a personal and professional point of view. We talked about the attitudes that young people have today, as opposed to those that the young adults had years ago. He couldn't understand the mindset of the youngsters of today. What he got up to when he was a young man was nothing compared to what the young men of today do. The point he was making was that he, like the young men of his generation, knew when to stop. It was fascinating stuff. The only thing I'd forgotten about was how dreary it can be to transcribe such material.

I was on the lookout for another person to speak to. During the course of a conversation with my social worker, Louise, I told her what I was trying to do. She recommended somebody she knew who I could talk to. Once I had got myself organised, I went to meet this gentleman.

He lived in a part of the country that I had never been to before. On the day I left my house to meet him, the sun beamed. The train was virtually empty. When I got to my destination, this gentleman and his wife were waiting for me.

At their house, the couple offered me coffee and biscuits. I accepted them gladly. After sipping the coffee and nibbling at a biscuit, I began the interview.

Mr Evans' contribution was valuable. He had only worked at one school, but his comments turned out to be insightful. I thanked him for his help, and he took me back to the railway station.

Not long after carrying out this examination, I heard a phone-in on *The Customer* about young people. Apparently, a report had been written. What a coincidence.

In the meantime, at Westhampton Community Radio station, which was a part of Westhampton College, the station was making plans for the end of term. When the college closed, so did the radio station. It being the end of the academic year, the station planned to broadcast a special series of programmes. When we got round to doing our show, there was a lot of contention.

The station had scheduled a fifteen-minute news bulletin to be broadcast at the head of the programme. This meant my show would be reduced by fifteen minutes. Robert felt this was unfair. Gerry, who organised the broadcasting output for the station, pointed out that somebody would have to do a programme at this time. After a while, Robert saw his point of view. With this in mind, we recorded the show, but not without any difficulties.

We started to record, but the computer broke down. While Robert crawled under the desk to investigate the event, I wondered whether the programme would ever get going. Robert came out from beneath the desk and went upstairs to sort out the problem. Eventually, he came down, and the show got underway. In the end, it was successful. It occurred to me, however, that while we were making all this effort to record these programmes, I never heard them because I wasn't on the Internet.

During a conversation with one of my brothers, I learned there were Internet cafés that I could go to where I could listen to my shows. I investigated the matter and found a couple I could try. There was one which was particularly easy to get to. Over the past few weeks, I had been going there. The only thing that I didn't like was that the girls on reception were unable to find the station I wanted. Every time I visited the café, I had to wait for a chap called Colin to set up the computer for me. Luckily, he did not mind doing this. Nonetheless, on the day when I wanted to hear this special broadcast, Colin wasn't there.

July 2005

Before heading for the Internet café, I phoned to let them know I would be coming in. The person I spoke to assured me that somebody would be there who could help me. When I arrived, the receptionist said, "Colin isn't here, and there's nobody else who can set up the computer for you." I pointed out that I'd phoned to let them know that I was coming in. That didn't matter. I couldn't believe it! And I certainly could not hold back my anger! What was I going to do now? I stormed out of the café - wondering how I was going to hear my programme. I would have to miss it.

Just as I got to the end of the road, I remembered there was another Internet café in town, but I had no idea where it was. I strode off in the direction where I thought it was. It wasn't long before somebody offered to assist me. When I told him where I wanted to go, he had no idea where it was either. However, he helped me to find it. We walked and asked, walked and asked, and walked and asked, but nobody seemed to know where it was. In time, we found it, and we quickened our pace towards it. This Internet café wasn't like the other one. The first one often smelled of greasy food, whereas this one smelled of cigarettes. In a way, I preferred this Internet café because the manager put me in a back room, whereas at the other one, I always felt as though I was on display.

I was soon sitting at a computer. Fortunately, I had not missed much of my show. What I heard, I liked. Perhaps, in this case, it was a good job that the programme was headed by a long bulletin. This reflection reminded me that the other Internet café wasn't going to get away with the incident.

As soon as I got home, I rang the disability Rights Commission but I couldn't get through. I tried again, but nobody answered the phone. In the end, I contacted them first thing the following morning and got through. The person I spoke to gave me a complicated list of instructions. Basically, I had to write a letter of complaint first. I did, and in due course, I received a reply. Not only did they apologise for the event, but they also sent complimentary tickets for a meal.

August 2005

The internet café I used had rooms above it, and above those rooms was a restaurant. On the day I set out to meet my reader, who was going to be my guest, the sun beat down on us. We couldn't have wished for a better day. The restaurant, which was made of glass, was like a hot house. As we ate the fish we had ordered, we were bathed in heat from the sunlight streaming through the roof. No sooner had we left the building when the rain came down. We got drenched. At some point, I must have mentioned the incident to Robert because, not long afterwards, I heard an item on *The Customer* about somebody who had taken his case to the Disability Rights Commission. Should I have been attracted by this? I never knew. Later on, I would have more cause to wonder.

A friend of a friend recommended somebody else who I could interview. He was a retired headmaster. I arranged to meet him at one of the hotels in town. After we had ordered coffee, and it had arrived, I began to speak to this man. This gentleman had a wealth of experience. He had taught in a borstal, a semi-rural secondary school, and two community schools in the region. What he had to say was fascinating. From his interview, I could have written two articles. It took me a long time to transcribe this gentleman's comments. I wrote a proposal. Although I had never written anything like this before, I wanted to believe it would be successful, but other journalists did not.

September 2005

Once I was satisfied with the content of my piece, I asked my reader to email it to a newspaper. Before we knew it, they rejected it. I sent it to another newspaper that I had in mind. This paper turned it down too. Afterwards, I came to the conclusion that somebody must have scuppered the article. I really did feel as though I had been slashed in the face with a broken bottle.

You may well ask: how could somebody have blocked it? Louise Heart, the person who had put me in touch with Mr Evans, the first teacher I'd spoken to, worked at an organisation which was about to have a meeting with RAB. I knew this, because I'd been invited to attend, but I decided not to go. However, I know that I was mentioned because, when I went to the book club, reference was made to the fact that I had succeeded in getting an article published in a magazine. I had only told Louise about this. Clearly, somebody from RAB must have told BNUK about this. Despite this setback, I saw no reason why I shouldn't go ahead with my application to WMU (West Midlands University).

My next step was to write to the university to see what their attitude would be towards somebody like me - black, blind, and mature. Once again, I asked my reader to send an email on my behalf, but she did not receive a reply.

Two weeks later, I contacted the university, but the person I wanted to speak to wasn't available. A couple of days afterwards, WMU dispatched an email to my reader, saying, "It will be all right for you to go ahead with an application." It was with this in mind that I contacted WCR. I explained my intention to John and he agreed to help me.

Another application form came from DHDA. I filled it in and posted it. I also phoned DHDA and told them that I had already completed a form. Apparently, they had not received the first one that I had sent to them. There seemed to have been a mix-up over where the forms should have been addressed to. Still, they had no idea when the course would begin.

October 2005

Working with John was very different from working with Robert. At times, Robert could be tense, whereas John was much more laid-back. Also, John was more adept with the equipment. He was so skilled that I would go to the studio, read the script that I'd prepared, and go home afterwards. The equipment was so advanced that John could put the music in without us having to hear it. However, there was one thing I had to change about my programme - there would be no more discussion slot. At first, I dropped this because I didn't like the main story in the news that week - living wills - but after a while, it didn't seem appropriate or right.

Week by week, the programme began to take on a different shape. I focused more on the results of polls, surveys, and reports. *On This Day in History* became a regular feature. The only thing that was lacking was interviews.

Hurray! A letter came from DHDA inviting me to attend an induction session for the course. I couldn't believe it! The course was going to take place. The prediction had come true. I felt that, if everything went according to plan, I would be going somewhere.

When the day arrived to attend the induction, I thought I would never get there. I had arranged for the central heating to be serviced. The engineer came much later than I had thought he would. When he eventually turned up, he gave the system a thorough going over. Once he had finished, he pointed out several things that I would need to have done. At last, he was gone. I sighed a sigh of relief and made my way to DHDA.

It was seldom that I went to Hallam. My last visit was so long ago that there was now a new bus station in place. This meant that I had to get to DHDA via a different route from the one I remembered. As I walked along the street between the shops, I encountered a lot of street furniture. I could not recollect seeing this before. Further along the road, I came into contact with the market. I found myself walking through rows and rows of clothes. It definitely wasn't like this the last time when I had walked down this road. The road had been clear then.

When I got to DHDA, there were only two other people there - both of whom were women. One of the women had been doing the same as me throughout the year, phoning DHDA to find out what was going on. Like me, she had not got anywhere. The other woman who was present was more concerned about where she had parked her car. She left, saying that she was going to move it, but she didn't come back.

Meanwhile, the course administrator, Samuel, was busy pointing out why I couldn't do the course. He said, "You won't be able to see the lights going on and off in the studio." At WCR, this wasn't a problem. He also said, "You won't be able to climb the stairs to the studio." Ascending the stairs would not be a problem either. Besides, I had just scrambled up a flight of stairs to get into the building. He said, "I'll be in touch."

Back at home, I worried. Would they allow me to do the course? I waited, expecting to hear something, but nothing came. When the course started, I was there.

Before the course began, I had a week to fill. I was listening to *The Morning News* when I heard an item which caught my ear. It was a discussion about autobiographies - *Angela's Ashes* by Frank McCourt in particular. As funny as this might sound, I thought about the book I had been trying to write several years ago. It was about an experience I went through when I was studying on an access course. Have they got a copy of this book? It would not surprise me if they have. The version they would have obtained would have been an example of a work in progress. I've got the last edition of the book that I worked on. Only one other person has read it, and that was the woman who had commented on it. Was this an attempt at attracting my attention? It wouldn't be the last time I wondered about this.

November 2005

The course started today, and I went along. When I got to DHDA, the place was packed. Where had all these people come from? This large gathering of potential students shocked me because only two of us were at the induction. The room was so crammed that nobody could move even if we wanted. Eventually, a man stood in the doorway and told us to move into another room. This room was bigger, and most of us were able to sit down.

In time, the tutor entered, introducing himself as Tony. He explained what the course was about, the exercises we would have to do, and how it would be examined. Essentially, we had to attend regularly, write a fifteen-hundred word assignment, and record a broadcast we had made. It didn't sound too arduous, and I couldn't wait to get going. It was time for us to ask questions:

"What will happen when the course is over?"

"Will we get a placement?"

"What can we do with the certificate?"

These questions were answered and more besides. It was clear that, for some of the people present, this wasn't the sort of course they were looking for. Quite a few of the people there wanted to train to become a nightclub disc jockey.

Before I knew it, I was out on the street making my way towards the bus station.

The following evening, the room was packed again. Other people who did not show up the night before came. Tony explained what the course was about, but this time we managed to get some work done - or at least he asked us to do some. We had to find some information on the Internet. I wasn't able to carry out the search because the computers weren't accessible.

Nobody talked about offering me any support. Clearly, I was going to have to manage on my own, and I did. Whenever I needed to get information from the Internet, I would ask the staff at the library to download it for me. Once they had done this, I would send it to a woman who transcribed it into Braille. Throughout the duration of this course, I used this method, and it worked.

December 2005

Tony showed us the studio today. It was on the top floor of the building. The building we were in was tall, and it had the most unusual flight of stairs that I had ever seen. They were like a backwards S. I found them difficult to climb up and to come down. There was no way I could have either run up or run down them. I had to negotiate them with care.

There were several rooms off the landing. Immediately in front were the stairs which led up to the studio. They were narrow and steep but not too difficult to navigate. The studio itself was large and carpeted. Next to it was a kitchen.

As we presented our ten-minute programmes, taking it in turns to do so, we huddled around the broadcasting desk. Going to WCR had given me an advantage. I never felt embarrassed about what I was doing, and I didn't do anything wrong. The experience was much better than I had thought it would be, and I really did enjoy myself. There was, however, one black spot.

Often, Tony made comments that I didn't like. He got himself into knots when he talked about bullying. According to him, nobody should allow him or herself to be ill-treated. Why mention bullying anyway? It wasn't necessary. Every now and again, I wondered whether he had been talking to somebody about me. When this theme ran out of steam, he told us about the outcomes of doing this course, "Some of you," he would say, "will never make it to BNUK." Or, "You may get on to a course, but that won't guarantee you a job." I flinched whenever he made comments like this. I had no doubt in my mind that he was in contact with The Child.

Tony was far too decent a person to say things like this. He was a man who, in his own way, was highly regarded.

Tony came from the Caribbean. He used to work in the broadcasting industry over there. On coming to this country, he had gained a reputation for helping college students to fulfil their goals where getting into the media was concerned. According to him, he was always in the newspaper. This being the case, nastiness wasn't something I could attribute to him.

For some unknown reason, I phoned Gerald, another clairvoyant who conducted his readings over the phone. The only drawback with this was that clients had to tell him what it was they had in mind. Clairvoyancy ought to be about what the clairvoyant can see based on a person sitting in front of him or her. Be that as it may, it wasn't how Gerald worked. There was a time when Gerald's readings were always accurate. Not so now. Why?

Gerald told me, "The psychic experience that you suffered in 2003 was a genuine one. The person who should have contacted you, hesitated." My interpretation of this was that the person who should have got in touch with me, may have been afraid.

Somehow, I got the impression that Gerald had been talking to somebody about me. He suggested that I needed to know how to protect myself.

He described a visualisation exercise I should do before I went to sleep at night. I was to visualise a flower and rub my solar plexus at the same time. Later on, I came across other ways of protecting myself such as imagining breathing in gold and wrapping a cloak around myself. The idea was that these actions should prevent me from receiving thoughts on what clairvoyants call the astral.

I asked Gerald about the sensations I experienced. He said, "They're indicators of a psychic ability, but I don't think they're well developed." He thought that I should interpret them in the way I understood them. Furthermore, he advised me not to be distracted by them. What I would like to know is this: what did he tell BNUK? I don't know why, but I suspected he was suspicious about the whole thing. In many respects, I could see why. The response that I should have received should have been automatic, like a reflex action.

It should not have been an action that formed part of a conversation two and a half years later.

Gerald predicted that I would get on to the course I wanted.

Naturally, this was the outcome I hoped for. But would I?

2006

January 2006

A new year and a new hope - but what would the year bring? A lot - so I hoped.

At the beginning of this year, I had the feeling that one of the female presenters on *The Morning News* had done something against me. I certainly felt that I had an enemy.

Back at DHDA, only two of us turned up. I shouldn't have been surprised by this, but I was. Ever since the first night, numbers had been falling. But two of us? Things must have been bad.

Where the course was concerned, we weren't being asked to do anything that was too arduous. The truth of the matter was, it was a pity. Here was an opportunity primarily for black people, and they weren't interested in taking advantage of it. Maybe two evenings a week during the winter was asking too much. Perhaps, for some of those who had come along, it just wasn't what they wanted. For others, this course may not have fitted in with their lifestyle at this point in their lives.

Timothy and I arrived clutching our playlists and presented whatever we had prepared. In a way, it was a good job there was only two of us there. We didn't have to worry about taking up too much time. We did what we had to do, then we left. I didn't stop to think how the course could run with just two people on it. It was running, and that was all that mattered.

Meanwhile, I was still going to WCR. I was continuing to enjoy presenting the weekly show of music and news. The only change that had taken place was that I was now broadcasting the programme live. This was a move in the right direction, and I felt fortunate that John could spare the time to help me to do so. He introduced me to somebody who he thought could assist me. She was a woman who had come from Iran. Her name was Yass. She was a sweet person, but I found it difficult to understand what she was saying. This was not helped by the fact that some of the groups had weird names. Consequently, I never established a working relationship with this woman, but she often operated the desk under John's supervision. At the back of my mind was the course at WMU.

I really wanted to apply for it. Before I did so, I checked with the course leader if I could use either John or Tony as a referee. It had been twelve years ago since I had gone to university. The course tutor, Linda Hunt agreed, and towards the end of January, I submitted an application, together with an article that I had read onto a cassette. I had come across a couple of short pieces in a newspaper, and I thought one of them would be suitable.

Shortly after I had sent in my application form for a place at WMU, I received a letter granting me an interview. I could not help but smile to myself. But how could I find out what the examination would involve? I rang the university itself in a bid to find out, but the person I spoke to wasn't very supportive. I had no idea where to begin with regard to preparing for the interview. I would just have to do as well as I possibly could.

Not knowing how to get ready, I wasn't sure whether to take my Perkins Brailler with me. It was heavy and cumbersome to carry. Ultimately, I decided to take it. Nothing would be worse than being presented with a writing exercise and not being able to do it.

February 2006

On the day in question, I set out in plenty of time. I had to catch two buses. I encountered no problems with the journey. When I got to the university, somebody helped me to find the room where I needed to be. Other candidates had already arrived. It felt good - being there.

Linda Hunt and her colleague came into the room and, after they had greeted us, the interview day got underway. It was an open interview, and soon it was my turn to be grilled. So far as I can recall, I answered the questions as well as I could. Judging by the way Linda Hunt responded when I described the programme I presented at WCR, she wasn't impressed. Nobody had ever said that what I was doing there was wrong.

When this part of the meeting was over, Linda Hunt led us into a room where we had to practise reading a news bulletin.

The university had not arranged for a copy of this to be available in Braille, so one of the other candidates volunteered to read it to me while I Brailled it. It didn't take us long to transcribe it, but the other candidates marvelled at the woman who had helped me. When we had finished, I tried my best to concentrate on perusing the news report. It wasn't easy because the room was noisy with other candidates practising the same task. Eventually, it was my turn to read the bulletin.

I started off very well, but soon faltered. A wave of relief passed over me when it was over. After perusing the news report, I had to do a current affairs test. Because the university had not provided a copy of this in Braille either, I ended up having to dictate my answers to Linda Hunt herself, who recorded them. I didn't think this was an ideal way to do this exercise, but in the circumstances the arrangement would have to suffice.

It was a difficult test. I thought I listened to the news and took on board what was happening in the world, but not according to this exercise. I had never heard anything about some of the questions that were asked. As for the three theory-type questions, I had no idea what they related to, which bothered me. The thirty minutes allotted for this test was over, and it was time for lunch.

In the canteen, I had a tasteless sandwich and a drink. There wasn't much time allocated for lunch. We ate in haste and went back to the room in time to start the afternoon session.

The last exercise we had to do was the headlines. The girl who had read the news bulletin to me also had had the presence of mind to read this test. Linda Hunt told us that the headlines would be a controversial exercise. It wasn't a contentious exercise in the group I was attached to. We organised the headlines as well as we could and waited for our turn to explain why we made the decisions we had.

We didn't get the order right, but then I don't think any of the other teams did either. I had a feeling that this was one of those tasks that would come with practice. The interview was almost at an end. After we had asked many questions, Linda Hunt explained the next step — the outcomes that were on offer: "You will either receive an acceptance letter, a rejection letter or be placed on a reserve list. If you're put on the reserve list, you will only receive an offer if somebody drops out." As I left the building, it occurred to me that one day can make all the difference to somebody's life.

Two days later, I received a letter from the university saying, "We have put your name on our reserve list." I wasn't sure how to regard this placing – was it good or bad? Only time would tell.

WCR gave me another hour to present my show. It came as a complete surprise to me, and I felt flattered. The programme I broadcast had a definite structure to it. In the first hour, I presented items about education, business and the environment. Also, I would do *On this Day in History*. In the second hour, I broadcast pieces on health, auctions, and awareness days. I liked the programme I presented. The only things that were missing was interviews.

In the meantime, DHDA had obtained an RSL (restricted service license).

March 2006

The announcement that DHDA had been granted an RSL was sudden, even though it was what we were expecting. It was one of those situations where, although we knew it was coming, we had not prepared for it. I think this was because only two of us were attending the course on a regular basis. I had thought of lots of things I wanted to do, but I hadn't been encouraged to think about them. Consequently, I hadn't prepared anything, but something needed to be planned, and quickly.

Kneeling on my living room floor, I was surrounded by a mound of CDs. I was beginning the process of writing a playlist. It was a laborious task, and it was a good job that I had taken the trouble to Braille the inlays of my CDs before I had gone to WCR. Using these lists where I could, I selected songs, checked that I had got the right track number by using my talking book machine, then I made a note of it. In this way, I compiled a playlist, and when I had finished it, I word processed it. After I had done that, I produced both a Braille and print copy of the list.

The first show I presented went very well. DHDA delivered. The agency had found somebody who could be with me when I broadcast my programmes. B was an Asian woman, and I believe she was into dance music and would often act as a DJ at nightclubs. With B by my side, I presented my first live show on FM. Although I had done this for WCR, somehow this experience felt more real. This station was broadcasting to a wider audience, covering a larger area. After I had arranged my maiden show, I went on to prepare themed programmes.

The first of these shows involved playing music sung by female singers. It was a good idea, and it worked well. The only problem with this programme was that I had not planned enough tracks. Fortunately, one of the compilation discs I was using had other songs by female artists on it, which I had not used. As a result of this, no one will ever know how grateful I was to compilation discs.

The next themed programme I arranged was a reggae show. In order to prepare for this programme, I asked members of my family if they had any reggae CDs I could use. One of my brothers came up trumps. Using these, together with some of the tracks that I already had, I planned another show.

I had to fight to present this programme. Somehow, there had been a mix-up about who was going to broadcast a show on a Sunday afternoon. I knew that I would never get an opportunity to do this again, so I stood my ground. How the dispute came about, I will never know, because I was scheduled to do it in the first place. Once more, this went extremely well, and I really did feel supported by the people around me.

The final themed programme that I arranged was a seventies show. Once again, I waded through my CDs looking for all of the seventies tracks I could find. I produced a list.

The day on which I presented this programme, turned out to be the very last time I would be able to do a show. I thanked B for the help she had given to me by giving her a box of chocolates. She had not expected this at all.

On this particular occasion, B did not support me as well as she had been doing. There was a lot going on in the studio, in the form of people coming in and going out. Somebody who she had not seen in a long while turned up and she had to catch up with him.

Eventually, my time was up. I felt as though an era had come to an end. I would probably never see any of these people again. Of course, I had every intention of taking people's names and addresses, but I just didn't get around to doing it. I said my goodbyes and hoped I was walking up Hallam High Street for the last time.

As soon as I got home, I realised I would have to go back to hand in my folder. The folder had to contain a recording of one of the programmes I had broadcast and an assignment.

By this time, several weeks had elapsed since my interview at WMU.

I toyed with the idea of contacting Linda Hunt and turned it down.

One day, I plucked up the courage and phoned her. One of the things I noticed straight away was how hostile she sounded. When I asked her if anything had been decided, she went on to explain why they had put me on a reserve list, "We thought that you had something else to do."

If I had something else to do, I would hardly have applied for a place on the course. I sighed a sigh of relief when this conversation was over. Clearly, she didn't want to have anything to do with me. What had I done to be so despised? I contacted Gerald.

Gerald seemed to think that, even though I had taken my Brailler to the meeting, Linda Hunt had not taken me seriously. However, I was not to worry at this stage because nobody had received an offer.

The process was still ongoing. Some students were considering going to other universities, and one applicant was pregnant. Gerald thought that I would hear something favorable in a few weeks' time. This news cheered me up. I really wanted to believe this would happen. But would it?

For some inexplicable reason, the idea of considering another university came into my mind. This was the last thing I wanted to do. WMU was on my doorstep. It would be so convenient to get to. But would they give me the chance to go there?

April 2006

Before I could get in touch with Trentford, the other university I had in mind, I would have to find out where I stood with regard to money. Earlier in the year, I had heard so much talk about fraud; it was the last thing of which I wanted to be accused. I contacted a helpline only to be told that I would not be breaking the law. This meant that I could get in touch with Trentford University, if I wanted.

I told John of my intention and asked him to keep quiet about it. On learning that there were places at Trentford University, I requested an application form and information pack.

When the material came through, I noticed there was a test I had to do. Using the information supplied, I had to write three short news stories, put them into a running order, and then read them onto a blank cassette. I did this, and completed the form.

When I went back to WCR after Easter, John filled out the reference sheet. Before posting the application, I held on to it. There was still a possibility that I might hear from WMU, even though it was not long before that course was due to begin. I considered ringing Linda Hunt again but could not bear to hear that icy voice.

In the midst of all of this, I had an idea: I could find out what was going on when I handed in my folder containing the assignment that would be examined. On the day when I set out to go to DHDA to deliver my work, I could feel the warmth of the sun on my face. Samuel was in his little room upstairs. He invited me to sit down, and as I did so, I explained why I had come to see him. I gave him my folder, and he thanked me for it. After a pause, I broached the subject I wanted to talk about, "Has BNUK been in touch with DHDA about me?" Samuel either did not understand my question because he is African, or he just didn't want to answer it. I didn't receive a reply, even though I asked him the same question a second time. Realising that I wasn't going to get anywhere with him, I left his little room.

May 2006

I heard nothing more from WMU. Either the places had all been taken, or they just didn't want me on their course.

When I spoke to Gerald, he said, "You've been prevented from getting on to the course at WMU." I mentioned my intention to go to Trentford. He was sceptical, as I would have to move. I appreciated what he was saying, but I had not gained a place at WMU. He hinted that perhaps I should reapply to WMU next year. This was an idea I had not thought about. He commented on the fact that the person who should have been helping me was unwilling to do so. However, if I got a place at Trentford University, he believed that people would forget about me.

The Unfulfilled Promise

Around about this time, I kept on hearing references to Trentford on BNUK, whether it was in the form of an academic being interviewed about his expertise in a particular field, or in the sense that more stories were being reported from the area. Had somebody said something about the fact that I'd applied for a place there? If somebody had, who was it John or Gerald?

At this stage, I wasn't concerned about the idea that other people may have found out what I was doing because it did not occur to me then that somebody could cause mischief. Besides, it never really crossed my mind that somebody like Gerald would broadcast the contents of our conversations. Surely, they were just between him and me.

Before I ended my conversation with Gerald, he said a most curious thing, "The Child has set up a spy base." At the time, I thought the person who had told Gerald this was amused by the idea. I didn't know what he meant, but I was soon to find out, and be alarmed by it.

A letter came from Trentford University inviting me to attend an interview. I could not contain my joy. This would make up for not getting a place at WMU. I filled in the slip saying that I would come to the meeting, but two days before I was due to go, somebody from the university phoned me. The person said, "We've postponed your interview. There won't be enough time to get the general knowledge test transcribed into Braille." According to the messenger, "You shouldn't have received a printed letter because you declared that you are a registered blind person."

What could I do? Nothing! It shocked me that a meeting could be put off for such a reason. How long would it have taken to transcribe twenty questions and half an A4 page?

Meanwhile, I tried to get in contact with Robert. I had not heard from him since March, when he told me that his father had died.

One night, I had a dream about Robert. In the dream, he was very happy. Later on the following day, he phoned me. He apologised for not getting in touch with me sooner, but he had had tennis elbow. He was in a very good mood. He challenged me to ask him anything I wanted to know. I asked him about news theory. He told me about this in a sentence or two. He urged me to ask him something else. I had never known him to be in such a playful and jolly mood. What had brought it on? An idea did spring to my mind, but I said nothing.

June 2006

A woman from Trentford University phoned me. She wanted to know whether I had filled in a form stating what my needs would be as a registered blind person. I told her that I had completed and returned such a form. She sounded as though she did not believe what I was saying. Of course, I had sent it back.

Why on earth wouldn't I have done so? I wondered whether anyone had tampered with the form in the post. Possibly, possibly not.

I visited the counsellor again. I had not seen him since I told him that I'd gained a place at DHDA. He hadn't been pleased to hear my news. It was all right to get involved with radio, so long as it wasn't going anywhere.

It was a strange consultation, which cost sixty-five pounds. It was unusual because he wanted to hear how this radio business had come about. I told him the entire story.

I said, "I don't think the experience is an aberration." This was because I kept on hearing things associated with the programme I presented, "Hello and welcome." This was how I started my own show at WCR. At first when I heard, "Hello and welcome," I didn't like it. With time, I had to face the fact that, once these things are broadcast, anyone can say them. Later on, I heard a variant of, "have a good week." This was the phrase I used to end my shows.

Something had happened to trigger this psychic experience, but in the absence of a response, I couldn't prove anything in a concrete way.

He asked, "What would it take for you to believe there's something in the claim you've made?"

"I want to be told," I said. "I longed to hear somebody say..." I really believed it was about guidance, but I had not received any. So far as I was concerned, I had left the matter alone, and I meant every word that I said. Suddenly, I realised that I had not said what I had come to say. I wanted to tell him that I was going for an interview at Trentford University. I ended up leaving his consulting room feeling that, in some way, I had been cheated out of my reason for coming.

I had a preternatural feeling as I lay in my bed that night - a feeling that the counselor had recorded the consultation. Why? What for?

I set out in plenty of time to catch the train to Trentford. Once at Trentford, I took a taxi to the university. I was too early and had to wait. It was quiet. Not many people were about. The next candidate arrived – a young woman who wasn't very talkative. Another candidate turned up. This time, it was a young man who had a lot to say. The lecturer came and he guided us upstairs and told us about the course. He also gave us the opportunity to ask questions. We all asked questions, and the lecturer seemed to be pleased about this. When that part of the day was over, he whisked me off on a tour of the broadcasting centre.

The lecturer led me into a television studio. This didn't mean anything to me. I had not considered working in television. In many respects, it wouldn't be practical for a blind person to work in such an environment. In the radio studio, I looked around and felt more at home there. The lecturer showed me workstations. Once we had concluded the tour, the lecturer directed me into a little room where I had to do a journalism test. Writing news stories was new to me. I panicked a little, in case I wouldn't complete the exercise in time, but I did. Then I tackled the general knowledge test. I answered as many questions as well as I could, and ended up finishing the exercise bang on time.

After I had done this, the lecturer said, "I want to talk to you about your application." Talk – he did nothing of the sort. He interrogated me instead:

"Why do you want to do this course?"

"Why have you applied to this university?"

"Why do you want to be a presenter?"

"Why do you listen to BNUK?" (How would he have known that?)

These were the questions he asked over and over again, and he was never satisfied with the answers I had given to him. It was obvious he had been prejudiced against me. He wanted to know how I had got involved with radio. I told him, but I gave my story a new beginning. I could tell that this wasn't what he wanted to hear.

After what seemed like an age, he brought the interview to a close, and I had to speak to the people responsible for students with a disability. My feeling about this part of the day was that it was demeaning. While on the one hand I could see the necessity to find out what my needs would be, the detail they went into made me feel like a burden. What course administrator wants to know they are taking on somebody who could be more trouble than they had anticipated? This was reflected in the lecturer's attitude as the meeting progressed. Everything had to be considered, and it made the process of taking on a disabled student seem more like hard work than a pleasure. (Ironically, once support is put in place, the student shouldn't experience any difficulties).

The lecturer left before the interview was over. He said, "I've got another meeting to go to. There's little I can add to what's being sought." Not long after he had departed, the interview broke up. I couldn't get on to my train quickly enough after this.

The outcome of the meeting took a long time to come through. I phoned the university twice to find out what was going on, but nobody could answer my question.

July 2006

It was on a Monday morning, three weeks after I had attended the interview, when I contacted the disability unit. If a decision had been made, they would know because the unit would have to produce a Braille version of the letter. I was right. They did know the result, and it was another rejection.

According to the letter, "You're too focused on wanting to be a presenter." That wasn't true. My purpose in applying for a place on the course was to broaden the experience I had – not to fine-tune one aspect of what I had already done. When I spoke to the lecturer a few days afterwards, I told him so. I thought the conclusion he had come to was unfair. For some unknown reason, I had a feeling that Robert — perhaps everybody — knew the outcome of the interview before I did. He probably even knew the real reason why I had been turned down. He seemed to think that I had used inappropriate language - talking about my desire to get into the media, as opposed to saying that I wanted to be a broadcast journalist. He appeared to doubt that I had written that I hoped to broaden the experience I had gained. Whether he believed what I said - that applying to Trentford was not entirely about wanting to be a presenter – I couldn't say. He seemed to think that the decision to turn me down was wrong and that it ought to be challenged. He didn't explain why, but he offered more than once to help me to write a letter to the university. The only problem I had with this idea was I didn't know the grounds on which to contest the judgement.

For all of Robert's solicitude over the rejection I had received from Trentford University, he wasn't so caring when I mentioned that I was going to apply for a traineeship with IBN.

Before I had gone to Trentford University, my reader had left a message saying, "There's a traineeship for a researcher available with IBN." The following day, I popped into the library and asked one of the librarians to look up the information on the website. She couldn't find it because I should have registered in order to get it.

The weekend before the application needed to be in, Frances and I were summoned to visit our sister, Martha, who was supposedly depressed because she was no longer going out with her rich boyfriend. When we got to her house, we found, rather than signs of depression, a sister who was determined to drag us from one house to another in her bid to find a new one. By Sunday morning, my tolerance level was running low, and I wanted to go home, but Frances wasn't ready. We began to argue, and when at last she decided to go, the car wouldn't start. She called the AA, who came out quite quickly, after which we were on our way home.

As soon as I got home, I was out again — on my way to my reader's house to get the information which would enable me to apply for the traineeship.

The Unfulfilled Promise

Armed with the necessary material, I started to work on the application. On the day of the closing date, I submitted the form. But, in many respects, it may have been too late because I had no doubt in my mind that Robert had told the people at BNUK about it, and I would have been disqualified as a consequence.

What was I going to do now? I remembered that I hadn't heard from DHDA. When I phoned the agency, the person who dealt with my call told me, "The results have not yet come out, and we don't know when they will." Something that Gerald had said came into my mind. I could reapply to WMU. I rang Linda Hunt. I did not hesitate this time. The woman I spoke to was very different from the one I had conversed with earlier in the year.

Linda Hunt said, "You can reapply," and she told me what she wanted me to do. One of the things she mentioned was a work placement at BNUK Central. She got somebody from that station to contact me.

When I spoke to the person who got in touch, he said, "You'll have to write a one-page critique of a show broadcast on the station." I knew which programme I would review and set about listening to the show.

It was a three-hour programme, and I listened to it every day for a fortnight, making notes as I did so. There wasn't much to criticise. When I had finished writing my report, I thought it would enable me to get a placement. I asked Robert if he wanted to hear it. He said that he did. He wasn't overflowing with praise, but he didn't condemn it either. I posted it, believing it would do the job.

Good news! I passed the course that I had taken at DHDA. I told Robert, who expressed his delight. He said, "You can get yourself on to a placement with that." I knew this, but getting a placement was already in hand. Perhaps, for the first time, I realised how much he would have liked to work at BNUK.

August 2006

I had a dream in which I saw one of the female presenters from *The Morning News*.

On *The Morning News*, on the day when my letter would have been received by BNUK Central, I heard a broadcast which sounded like what I had written in my critique. But how could BNUK have got hold of it? It wasn't possible. The only thing I could think of was that Robert must have recorded it. It didn't sound likely, but it certainly wasn't unlikely either.

Linda Hunt wanted me to do something else: join another radio station so that I could gain experience in a different working environment. I got in touch with the station she had recommended. As soon as I said, "I'm registered blind," the person I was speaking to didn't want to know. He accused me of deceiving him because I hadn't mentioned it straight away. I wrote and spoke to the manager who said, "I'll invite you to a forthcoming open day," but I never heard from him again.

The book club was still meeting throughout this time. There were times when I considered leaving but reflected that that would not be a good idea. I had already stopped going to the social club, but I wasn't going to allow anyone to drive me away from the book club, just because people were inclined to say tactless things and repeat comments they didn't understand.

This month, we read a fantastic novel, *The Kite Runner* by Khaled Hosseini. I got into it straight away. I really did like it and said as much at the book club. A few days later, I heard a piece on *The Morning News* about redemption — one of the themes in the novel. I accepted this book was not the only work with redemption as a theme, but in view of the fact that we had only just read it in the book club... Was it a coincidence, or wasn't it? Was it designed to attract my attention?

My thoughts turned to buying a new computer. I had been thinking about doing so for a long time but never had the money.

Now that I was considering doing a university course, I thought it would be a good idea to get one. The only problem I had was trying to work out what equipment would be suitable for my needs.

Great advances in technology had taken place over the years where computerised equipment was concerned. Today, blind people can buy a QWERTY keyboard with a screen that shows what is on it in Braille and/or in speech. This system is also available using a Braille keyboard, which also has a Braille screen and\or a speech system. These tend to be portable, whereas the QWERTY keyboards are either portable or desktop. I knew I was looking for something portable. Once I had stored information on it, I could transfer it to my desktop. I really needed to know what portable equipment would be compatible with the screen reader and the software I would be using on my computer.

In order to find out, I telephoned RAB. The first comment the person I spoke to made was that I didn't have to worry because I would get money to buy the equipment I needed. I knew this, but would it be enough? Then he said, "You won't be going to university."

Who was he to say? What did he know? Then it dawned on me. He had probably been talking to The Child or at least he had access to what he was saying. After all, RAB had links with BNUK.

September 2006

Hurray! My critique was successful. BNUK Central offered me a week's work placement. I couldn't believe it! I wanted to share my news with somebody, so I phoned Robert. He wasn't in. I left him a message. When he got in touch and I told him, he wasn't as pleased as I had thought he would be. John wasn't overwhelmed either. Why? Between them, they had helped me to achieve this tiny milestone, yet neither of them felt able to express their delight for me.

An idea came into my mind. They had been led to believe that I wouldn't get it, or perhaps that I had not earned it. The person who might have encouraged them to believe this was somebody who wanted to be in control but wasn't. When Robert understood what I was saying, he saw that he had been deceived. As a consequence, I heard him speak in a way I would not have thought possible. He was so bitter. I knew he understood that The Child should have contacted me. Robert was offended. He had spied against me, hence the powerbase, only to discover that it was never necessary. Robert was a proud and sensitive young man, and making this discovery must have hurt him – just as much as being injected without any anaesthetic.

Around about this time, I had a strange experience. In a way, I think it shed light on my thoughts about The Child, with regard to getting a placement. I wouldn't say this was a premonition because I wasn't being warned. Someone was saying, "You're going to destroy me." Where did it come from? What did it mean? Was it the case that The Child was fearful about what might happen when I was at BNUK Central?

Once, Gerald had said, "There are some people who wouldn't like to see you get on without them." Did this apply in this instance? Who could say yea or nay?

The book club met again. The novel we were reading this month was *Barchester Towers* by Anthony Trollope. I had heard a dramatisation of this on the radio many years ago and could remember a particular scene very well. However, when I read it for the book club, I didn't like it and I said so. It didn't seem to be about much. Looking back,

I cannot understand what the problem was that I had had with the novel. It wasn't that bad.

Nevertheless, on *The Morning News,* the presenter and guests discussed the novel. They were considering what it was about. A coincidence too? Remember, one of the members of the book club was friendly with somebody at BNUK.

October 2006

Today was the day when I started my work experience at BNUK Central. It was like going to work again - making sure everything was ready from the night before. I woke up early and got dressed. The only thing I couldn't work out was which bus to get - the thirty-one minutes past or the forty-three. Obviously, the thirty-one would get me there much earlier, but the forty-three would get me there on time. I caught the forty-three, and the journey took much longer than I had thought it would. I was beginning to wonder if I would ever arrive because of the traffic. The journey should have taken forty minutes; instead, it took fifty- two. When I eventually arrived at the place where I wanted to be, I got off the bus and crossed over the road.

On the other side, I found that workmen had taken up the pavement. Fortunately, there was somebody on hand to offer me assistance. In fact, every day of that week, a passerby helped me to cover the part of the journey from when I crossed over the road up to the building itself. It was kind of all of those people to support me. I could have asserted my need to be independent and turned them all away, but sometimes it's judicious to accept help. Living with a disability does not have to be about always having to prove this or that. Acknowledging assistance is a sign that you have come to terms with your loss.

Once I was inside the building, a security guard took me to reception where I had to wait. The reception area seemed to be a large space – the sort of place that would have plants in it. The sofa I sat on was spacious and comfortable. I was sitting down for so long that I thought they'd forgotten about me. In time, somebody came and guided me into the biggest room I'd ever been into. The room was huge! I had no idea how many people worked in it. Would it be possible for a small group of people to have a private conversation without being overheard? A room of this size struck me as a place where a person would probably be anonymous. Was I right in suspecting that senior staff worked alongside junior ones? Or is that the nature of team working — the high-ranking work alongside the low? I supposed if I had to work in such an environment, I would get used to it. In fact, I did get used to it and to the people around me.

A woman called Maxine oversaw my placement. Once we had introduced ourselves to each other, we started to talk about the content of the programme for that morning. To my surprise, she planned much of the show on the day it went out. This was because this programme, like so many others, responded to whatever was in the news or to whichever report had been published. After we had discussed the makeup of the show, Maxine escorted me to another room.

Maxine did not explain where we were going, but I soon realised I was in the studio where the programme was going to be broadcast. In other words, I sat in the studio while the show went on air. It felt like a very large room. Considering that Maxine had planned much of the show an hour or so before it was broadcast, it went well. There was a wide variety of guests, and listeners rang in with a wide range of calls. I wasn't used to sitting in one place for three hours. At home, I moved from room to room, but here, I had to stay put. Before the show ended, a woman offered me a cup of coffee. I accepted it gladly. When the programme was over, Anna took me for my lunch.

The canteen was a large room too. I felt as though I had been left in the middle of it. I ate the sandwich I'd bought and listened to the sounds around me. Mainly, I heard people talking. I cannot recall being overwhelmed by any cooking smells, but at two o'clock, Anna picked me up and took me back to the large room- the production room.

Maxine didn't know what to do with me. She suggested that I could edit some programmes. I agreed to do it, even though the computer I used didn't have any speech on it. It had been a long time since I had typed anything without speech. If there were mistakes in it... In the end, it was either word-processing without speech or doing nothing.

One of the shows I checked was about a former chief executive of one of the building societies in the area. It was interesting. Somehow, I hadn't thought about somebody like this in that way. We tend only to think about the people who are pushed under our noses. When I had edited that one, I did another one about Daniel O'Donnell. Once I had checked this programme, it was time to go home.

The following day was Tuesday. Maxine led me into another room – the ops room. When I first entered this room, a noise hit me. What the sound was, I cannot say. It was loud and seemed out of order.

This was the room where the girls took the listeners' calls. From this room, Maxine communicated with the person presenting the show and presided over it. The atmosphere was invariably tense. I could scarcely hear what was going on in the studio. One of the women gave me the task of answering a white phone.

The calls came from reception, saying that such and such a guest had arrived and would somebody collect them. I spent the next two days in this room. On the final day, I was in the large, anonymous room again. At first, I made calls for Maxine, after which she introduced me to a woman called Brenda. I passed the rest of the morning with this woman. Brenda dealt with people who had services to offer callers with problems. She had a pleasant disposition, and she loved her cigarettes. Before settling into whatever it was she may have wanted me to do, there was something I had to do – make a phone call.

Earlier in the week, John from WCR had called me to ask if I could get in touch with him. I asked Brenda if it would be all right to use the phone. She said, "It will be." When I rang John, I received the shock of my life. He said, "Robert's dead." I couldn't believe what I had been told: Robert was dead. It didn't strike me as possible. He was so young – twenty-nine. That was no age to die. He had suffered an aneurysm. He had complained about headaches. He had been to the hospital, where they had given him the all clear. As soon as he had returned home to his flat, he had died. Alone. How awful.

The alarm had been raised when he didn't show up for work the following morning. This news stunned me. I couldn't believe it! I asked Brenda if I could speak to Gerry. Gerry had known about Robert's death for a few days. He had no idea when the funeral would be. We talked about Robert for some time, trying to put together what we knew about his life.

Robert loved radio. It was all he ever talked about. He had a sister who had been travelling in Australia. He told me about some of the photographs she had sent home. His mother, a psychologist, had died. His father was a philosophy teacher. According to Robert, his father hadn't been able to cope in a classroom situation, so he had given up on teaching. Earlier in the year, his father had passed away. He wasn't very old. Robert came from Cheshire, and he had an uncle in Norwich. This was the sum total of our knowledge about him. Aware of where I was, I ended the conversation and went back to what I should have been doing.

The Unfulfilled Promise

Maxine asked, "Have you heard the news?" I had not. I explained why. She may not have been impressed by the reason I had given to her. The long and short of it was, she wanted me to write another cue. Before I could do this, something extraordinary happened.

Brenda advocated that I should read the round-up for the desk that dealt with callers who had volunteered to help people in some way, on air. I really wanted to do it, so long as it would be allowed. Eventually, a producer granted me permission to do this. Brenda dictated the material I was going to read. Thank goodness I'd brought my mini Brailler with me. It had been in my bag all week. It was heavy, but now it was going to be used. I read through the piece a couple of times. Suddenly, it was time – time for me to go on air. How incredible! My hands shook. I was on air! I read the round-up, then I was off again. It was all over in a couple of minutes.

When I had done that, I wrote a cue. It was about Sir Richard Dannatt, who was calling for the army to pull out of Iraq. Once again, I showed it to Maxine, who said, "It's fine." Throughout the week, I had been writing cues, so I supposed I was a dab hand at them by now. It was almost time for me to leave.

Maxine gave me the contact details for Hallam Hospital Radio. Years ago, I went there, but I didn't have a positive experience.

At first, when I had gone to Hallam Hospital Radio, I visited the wards. But my experience soon deteriorated into turning up once a week, only to listen to the radio. I was not encouraged to do anything. It was dispiriting. The other difficulty I endured was over getting home. If the Asian girl was there, there was no problem; she would just give me a lift.

In order to get to the hospital, I needed to catch two buses. Getting to the hospital this way wasn't a problem, but going home was another matter altogether.

The way the buses were scheduled to run, I found that I would have to wait for half an hour in Hallam town centre. To avoid this, there was a bus I could get which would take me home, but this involved crossing a car park. The car park at Hallam Hospital Radio was not easy to negotiate, but nobody ever wanted to help me to cross it. So in the end, I left. That was the one and only time in my life when I had come across people who weren't willing to assist me.

When I contacted Hallam Hospital Radio again after my experience at BNUK Central, I spoke to Phil. He had helped me when I was at DHDA. I thought this would pave my way, but it didn't. I submitted a form, but I never heard from the hospital again. In my mind, I questioned whether they had ever received it. Although I went through the process of filling out a form, the person who acted as my amanuensis insisted on posting it. Did she put it in the mail bag?

I contacted other hospital radio stations. Many of them said that they wanted to carry out a criminal record check. This would have taken a very long time. Others just had answering machines. On one of these, I left my name and number and hoped.

The Customer was talking about silent calls. I listened. The presenter and guest went on to discuss TPS (Telephone Preference Service). They sounded as though they were enjoying the conversation. Was this a way of confirming my suspicion?

Before I had gone to BNUK Central, I had a funny feeling one morning. This was followed by an anonymous call. I rang 1471, but the caller did not leave a number. I put the experience out of my mind. When I came home from BNUK Central on Thursday and Friday, I noticed that a marketing company was trying to get in touch with me. This was unusual because companies don't pester people. I should know. I've been at home for several years, and I've never experienced this before. As strange as I thought it was, I dismissed it. If I dialled the number to find out who it was, I would have been given another number to call.

On the following Monday, the telephone rang. When I picked up the handset, nobody was there. I keyed in 1471 and discovered it was the same number where the calls I received last week came from. I put the handset down. Just as I got settled into sorting out some rubbish, the phone rang again. I answered it, only to find that nobody was there. It was the same number.

After these calls, I received a few more from this number. I probably responded to about six anonymous calls in total that day. I made a note of the number. When I dialled it, I found it was a marketing company or, to be more precise, a market research company. And, in order to get through, I would have to ring another number. The following morning, I had reported the matter to TPS.

On hearing this discussion about silent calls, I was reminded that, in the summer of the previous year, I had received an anonymous call. At that time, I wondered whether it was The Child. Hearing this report now left me in no doubt that it was him who had made that call, and the more recent ones. There was one thing that was certain: Although the calls had come from a marketing company, they certainly weren't random. They were deliberate. But what could I do about the situation? I couldn't ring up and complain about receiving the calls because it would have been denied.

I knew I wouldn't make it to Robert's funeral, so I arranged for a white cross to be sent to WCR. The contingent who went to the funeral from there took the flowers with them to the crematorium in Cheshire.

I thought about Robert on the day and knew that I would miss him very much.

November 2006

Roger, the manager of the hospital radio station at Wall Heath, phoned me. He invited me to attend an interview. How wonderful. After finding out how to get to Wall Heath Hospital, I set out to go to the meeting.

Considering it was November, I did not have to wear a hat, gloves or a scarf. Getting into Wall Heath itself wasn't a problem. Somebody helped me to locate the stand I wanted in order to get a bus that would take me to the hospital. When I got off the bus, I found that I had not been dropped off outside the right entrance. A woman called Christine came to my rescue. With her support, I got to the station, where I met Roger. I told him about the work I had done and why I wanted to get involved with Wall Heath Hospital Radio. He listened. After thinking about my request, he said, "You can join the station, but you'll have to find your own assistance." I agreed to his terms, thanked him, and left.

On the way home, I wondered who I could get to help me. I thought about B, who had assisted me when I was at DHDA. Samuel gave me her number, but when I phoned her, she wasn't available. I racked my brains to see who else could help me, and I came up with my sister's boyfriend Stephen, who, at that time, wasn't working. He offered to support me, and for a few weeks, he did the necessary training.

In the book club, we read *The Constant Gardener* by John Le Carré. It wasn't what I was expecting. If somebody had told me what it was about, I would have dismissed it. But once I got into it, I couldn't put it down. Justin was so courageous. To my amazement, I heard an interview about an aspect of this story on *The Morning News*.

Another coincidence? I read somewhere that too many concurrences equals a plot. Was there a plan? If there was, what was it about?

My mind was made up. I was going to order a computer. I wrote to the company, enclosing a cheque with the letter. Ten days after I had sent this letter, nothing had come. A manager had told me, "It will take ten days to arrive." On the eleventh day, I phoned the firm to find out what was going on. The sales assistant said, "There's a shipping problem." Seven days later, the computer arrived. When it came to putting it together, I found that it had a large monitor – as big as a television screen. Toby, my brother, told me to ask for a smaller one. When I got in touch with the company, the woman I spoke to sounded angry. Why? It was almost as though I should never have had the computer in the first place. I wondered if an attempt had been made to stop the purchase. It was a ridiculous idea. Reluctantly, the angry woman agreed that I could change the monitor, but I would have to pay extra for it.

Months later, I detected a note of relief when I contacted the company. It was as though they realised they would have lost out on a sale if the plan had gone ahead. So, it wasn't my imagination. There had really been an attempt to prevent the purchase.

December 2006

For some unknown reason, I went to see another clairvoyant, Raymond. I didn't know what I was looking for, but I thought I'd found something.

One of the first things Raymond said was, "You're going to receive a phone call." I told him that I wouldn't. He refuted this claim, but I insisted that I would not. According to Raymond, "Somebody will contact you because he's got some information to pass on to you that will be beneficial." I didn't receive the call. This did not surprise me.

Then he said something which really baffled me. He seemed to be suggesting that I had come to the wrong conclusion. At the time, it occurred to me that somebody was being protected. At first, I couldn't think what he was referring to. One day, it dawned on me. He was alluding to something that I had said in the consultation with the counsellor.

My assertion that The Child was trying to blackmail me did not go down too well. In part, I think it was because nobody understood why I made the claim that I did. I think people thought I was being nasty. Nobody understood that I received a warning. It really was The Child's intention to blackmail me. When he drew on the experience I went through with the Civil Service, this was exactly what he was doing. Faced with the remarks I made, of course, he would deny it, but I knew I was right. He had never imagined that I would find out about his thought processes.

Raymond said something else which puzzled me. He seemed to be insinuating that nobody paid attention to anything I said. Was this because the explanation I had given during the consultation was ignored? It sounded as though he was intimating that I did have something worthwhile to say, but nobody wanted to hear it. Was he alluding to the fact that nobody wanted to hear that I had left the matter alone? That would be about right. It would take me a long time to work out the point he was trying to convey. On the other hand, he could have been referring to the book club. Later, I came to the conclusion that certain members of the group may have been asked to record the meetings.

Then Raymond commented on the interview that I had attended earlier in the year at WMU. According to him, "You weren't prepared for it." I knew I wasn't ready for it. Unlike some of the other candidates who were there, I did not know anybody from whom I could have got tips. I could have asked Robert, but he phoned, saying, "You won't hear from me for a while because my father's ill." Ultimately, it was a case of going to the interview or not going to it. This criticism made me realise one thing: At some point, Linda Hunt must have given certain people the opportunity to listen to the part of the interview she recorded - the current affairs test. Later, some BNUK presenters poked fun at the way I spoke – the fact that I had hesitated. After the criticism came the praise.

Raymond went on to say, "You've done very well, and you should be proud of what you have accomplished." At first, I couldn't understand the achievement he was talking about. On reflection, I realised he was talking about going to university. At least, I came to the conclusion that he must have meant this because my sister made a comment along the same lines.

At the time, my sister, Martha, who is a headmistress at a primary school, was making a programme with IBN. Through this link, other members of my family became implicated in this affair, but not one of them felt it was their duty to explain the chicanery with which they were involved. They were more than happy to take part in what could only be described as an attack on me.

If the activities that BNUK went on to do was about help, I would like to know how they would have behaved if they weren't supporting somebody? They were merciless in what they went on to do, and all I could do was bear it with as much fortitude as I could muster.

Stephen finished the training. This meant we could start doing the programmes at Wall Heath Hospital Radio whenever we liked.

2007

January 2007

A new year and a new hope – but what will the year bring? Success - I hoped.

This year started with a morning in hospital. For as long as I can remember, I have always had a cyst on my abdomen, which did not bother me until four years ago, when I went on a walking holiday.

A long-time friend, Sandra, who I had contacted out of the blue, asked me if I wanted to go on a holiday with her. At first, I hesitated, and then I agreed to go. I got in touch with the fellowship who was organising the holiday, and they told me how much it would cost and where it would be held. It turned out to be a most enjoyable week, but it started with an horrendous experience in London.

I had arranged to travel from Sandbury to Watford and then I would have to change trains. The train I would have got on would have taken me to my destination – Hurstpierpoint. At Watford, I was in the process of getting off the train when I heard the announcement for the train to Hurstpierpoint, being cancelled.

On alighting from the train, a member of the railway staff told me in no uncertain terms, "If you want to go to Brighton, you'll have to get the next train to London, where you'll be able to get a train to Hurstpierpoint." So, a few minutes after getting off one train which could have taken me to London, I boarded another one bound for the same destination. While I was on this train, I realised I would be late, and would probably miss being picked up. I tried to phone the people at the fellowship where I was going, but I couldn't get through. I kept on trying, but my efforts were in vain.

In the meantime, I arrived in London. I stepped off the train, but there was nobody around to help me. I didn't know what to do. A woman came to my rescue. She was on the train that I just got off and was going in the same direction as me. She offered to accompany me to Victoria station. Considering that I was carrying a large bag, which was cumbersome, we decided to get a taxi.

At Victoria station, the woman found a porter who was willing to assist me. He took me into the station, where I made an attempt to get somebody to get in touch with the station at Hurstpierpoint, with a view to letting the people who would be collecting me know that I'd be late. I believed somebody tried to make contact but without success. There was nothing more that I could do. I waited for my train, and when it came, a member of the railway staff helped me to board it. The woman who assisted me in London also got on the train, but she alighted before I did. I thanked her for her support and settled down to enjoy the rest of the journey. Eventually, I arrived at Hurstpierpoint, where a young man offered to carry my bag.

At the station, there was no one there to meet me. I phoned the fellowship to let them know where I was, and the person I spoke to said, "Somebody's on his way to pick you up." As soon as the driver appeared, he told me that someone came to collect me, but I wasn't at the station. The fellowship did not receive any messages saying that I would be late. I climbed into the minibus, and we were off.

At the fellowship, I met Sandra, who could not disguise her delight at seeing me again after all of this time. We were in the same room, but we did not have an opportunity to talk straight away. The fellowship will have planned for virtually every moment on a holiday like this. Before the activities of the following day got underway, we attended a service – a communion service in the chapel. It was a simple affair, which did not last for long because we needed to be on our way. When it ended, we set out to go to Lewes.

In Lewes, we rambled up and over the Sussex Downs by way of the South Downs. We walked until we arrived at a place called Ditchling Beacon. Along the way, we stopped and our guide told us about the Jack and Jill Windmills. We bought and ate ice creams. It was a day on which we could have left our jackets and coats behind, if we wanted.

Once we finished eating, we went back to the windmills where we consumed our tea. At this point, our guide gave the holidaymakers who did not want to do any more rambling the chance to go back to the fellowship. Those who weren't ready to go back went on to do some more walking. I was one of those who carried on rambling, and we walked to Hurstpierpoint.

On day two, we travelled by coach to a place called Yapton (south of Arundel). The people who led the walk, Brian and Carol, decided that it would be best for the ramble to be rerouted. When they did this, we found ourselves walking for several miles alongside the river Arun. The beach we rambled on was shingled. It was an easy, long walk, and we amused ourselves along the way. In the afternoon, our guides took us back to Yapton, where we ate our tea with The Little Hampton Fellowship in their village hall.

The fellowship went to a lot of trouble on our behalf. They made cakes for us and gave us tea. It was so kind of them. The choice of cakes was phenomenal. Most of us consumed as many of them as we possibly could. When we finished, we went back to where we were staying for a delicious supper.

On day three, we walked up Seven Sisters – a series of hills. They were quite steep. Nevertheless, we managed them very well. Apparently, the views along the way were stunning. At one point, the guides pointed out that they could see white cliffs and at another point, a meandering river in a valley below. To crown it all, it was another day on which we could have left our outer garments behind. We were blessed with the weather that week. For lunch, we stopped off near a National Trust shop. Outside, we sat under trees tucking into our packed lunches. Two of the people I was sitting near did nothing but complain. I thought this was a pity.

In the afternoon, we did another walk elsewhere. The name of the place was funny. During this ramble, an element of racing was taking place to see who could complete this walk first. I believe my guide and I were the first to finish this ramble.

On day four, we walked around Hurstpierpoint itself. This ramble became known as the Grand National. There were so many stiles we climbed over. Some people found this easier than others. At one point, a fellow walker fell into a ditch, pulling her guide on top of her. To this day, I cannot imagine how that could have happened, but at the time, it caused much laughter. Fortunately, neither of the people involved was hurt. This was a shorter walk than the ones we did earlier in the week. Before we knew it, we were back where we started.

For the first time during our stay at this place, the fellowship gave us an opportunity to explore the grounds. Many of us took the chance to see what they were like. The building was surrounded by a large garden, at the bottom of which was some sort of a house

– either a greenhouse or a summer house. Some of us took the time just to sit outside. Also, we ventured into rooms in the house that we did not know were there. The place was much bigger than we thought it was.

Day five saw us descending on Brighton. We were led by a tour guide on this trip. We stopped off at the pier where we saw a retired fisherman with his "dog fish." We visited museums, and we walked up and down the lanes. We took lunch at Brighton Pavilion Gardens. Afterwards, we went to a place called Rottingdean, which seemed to have associations with writers and artists. While we were there, we rambled around gardens and visited a church that received a stained-glass window as a donation. As if to keep us on our toes, our guide led us up a very steep hill, at the top of which was a windmill whose sails were recently restored.

On day six, we went to Devil's Dyke. At the bottom of this very steep hill, I consumed a bar of chocolate. Eating this treat powered me up the hill. As I climbed, a sense of elation passed over me. Evidently, my guide was fit and able - a woman from Burgess Hill. It was a good-natured walk, and we took part in a lot of light-hearted banter as we went. For a time, the ramble came to a halt because a bad- tempered dog was roaming around. As soon as he disappeared, our walk continued. We ate our lunch on a plateau. It was high up and afforded those who could see beautiful views of Sussex. I felt honoured that Sandra had invited me to take part in such a holiday.

As wonderful as this holiday had been, I noticed one thing: the cyst that had never bothered me before ballooned up like a ping-pong ball. It was massive and heavy. As soon as I got home, I went to the A & E Department at the hospital. The doctor who I saw said, "You've got an abscess, and it's a good job that you've come to see me." She lanced the abscess straight away. The next time I visited my GP, he thought it would be a good idea to have the cyst removed. But when I went to see the consultant, he couldn't find it. Three years later, the cyst reappeared, and I had to spend a morning in hospital.

I arrived at the hospital early and waited for somebody to take me up to the ward. While I lingered, I was struck by the number of people coming into the hospital. Who were they? Employees or patients or both? The stream was never ending. Eventually, a nurse took me upstairs where she introduced me to one of her colleagues. After all the bureaucracy had been completed, I waited to see the consultant. When he turned up, he questioned the necessity of having the cyst removed. I pointed out that it had already turned into an abscess once and that there was no reason why it shouldn't happen again. He grunted something and then he disappeared.

Two men came to take me into the operating theatre where the procedure would be conducted. Neither of them had any idea about how to guide a blind person. This discovery shocked me. In situations like this, you're at risk of an accident taking place. Basic training should be given as a matter of course. Leading a blind person is not difficult. On the contrary, it's very easy. Between these two men, they helped, albeit clumsily, to get me onto a trolley. Once I was there, the procedure began.

A member of the theatre staff anaesthetised the area that was going to be operated on. When she had done this, the surgeon inserted a cutting tool. I felt it. After I had indicated as much, he applied more anaesthetic. As he worked, the surgeon complained. According to him, "Today isn't a very good day. My operating load isn't very challenging." I supposed that that was how things were: at times, there would be minor ops to perform, while at others, he would have major surgeries to handle. It was just a matter of taking the rough with the smooth and the good with the bad.

He removed the cyst, and a porter took me back to the ward where I got dressed and waited for my instructions before leaving. The only order that a nurse gave to me was to visit the nurse at my GP's practice. Hurray! I was on my way home.

Now, I couldn't say where that cyst used to be. The procedure had been successful, but it never occurred to me that operations like this could be regarded as controversial. Not long after having my cyst removed, I heard a discussion on *The Morning News* about whether such procedures should be carried out. Naturally, I thought they should be. But was this just one of those things that happens, or was this more than a coincidence? Whatever the case, this debate reminded me there was a question I wanted to ask my sister, Martha.

After Christmas, Martha made a comment about something that she could only have known about if she had heard what Raymond had said in his reading, or if she knew someone who could have gained access to the recording. I made up my mind to tackle her about it. It was first thing on a Sunday morning when I phoned her. Sometimes early in the morning is the only time when you can find people.

Martha was in, and I wasted no time in getting to the point. According to her, "I've got no idea what you're talking about," yet she went on to accuse me of making up conspiracies. What connivances was she talking about? Was I in a position to conspire with anybody? No, I was not.

The conversation wasn't going anywhere, so I ended it. There were other things I had to think about – much more joyous things. One of them was my new radio programme, which was underway.

February 2007

At the beginning of the year, Stephen, my sister's boyfriend, helped me to get going on my new radio programme at Wall Heath Hospital Radio. It was going to be a very different show from the one I had presented at WCR. This one was called *The History File*.

The idea sprang from the realisation that Wall Heath had its own newspapers. It occurred to me that, if this was so, it would be a good idea to use this resource as a basis for a programme. When I investigated further, I discovered that Wall Heath had a local history centre. It held back copies of the local newspapers dating back to the nineteenth century. How tremendous! I assumed that most of the patients in the hospital came from the Wall Heath area.

This being the case, some of them might remember the stories I would be using. When the programme first got underway, it consisted of the history and meaning of place names in the Wall Heath area and notes on the history of the town, such as when the first bank had opened. Then there were two news stories, two sports stories, and two about entertainment. When I ran out of place names to use and historical notes on the town, I replaced these with *On this Day in History*. Every show was based around a particular year, and the music was taken from this time.

Although we were working at a hospital radio station, we weren't working in the traditional way - visiting the wards and picking up requests from the patients. Roger did not expect us to do this, partly, I think, because it was important to keep the station going. As a consequence, I did not receive any feedback from the patients about the programme. When I thought about it, I realised that I didn't have any feedback on the show I had presented at WCR either. Despite this failing, I continued to do the programmes because I regarded it as valuable experience. Also, it was what Linda Hunt had told me to do – go to another radio station to find out what working in another environment was like. This was exactly what I was doing.

The experience at Wall Heath Hospital Radio was certainly different from that at WCR. To start with, the studio was on the second floor. There were three sets of security doors to get through before entering the actual studio. The studio at WCR had the latest state-of-the-art equipment. This was not the case at Wall Heath Hospital. The equipment reminded me of the system that I had used when I started – a console and CD players. On several occasions, Stephen had difficulties with the play-out button and with the microphone. In spite of this, there was something comforting about Wall Heath.

The studio itself was not very large. It was long and narrow and so very hot. Perhaps, this was because it was at a hospital. There were times when the heat was overwhelming. Nevertheless, it didn't stop us from doing what we were there to do – present a show.

The oddest thing about working at Wall Heath was that we never saw another person. It was very seldom that the manager of the station would turn up and comment on what I was doing. On one occasion, he had given me a useful tip. Now and again, we encountered someone as we were entering the building, but that was rare. Later on, two young men came in after us to present a programme of sixties music. The extent of our conversation with these two men was, "Hello," and "Goodbye," and if Stephen had any problems with the equipment, he would let them know.

Strange as the situation was, I learned to get used to it. After doing the programme for six weeks, I got in touch with WMU because I wanted to be sure it would be all right to reapply for a place on the course. Looking back, I should have regarded Linda Hunt's words as a warning. Perhaps, because I was doing what I wanted to do, I hadn't picked up on the hints she had given to me. When I contacted her, she warned me not to talk about aiming to be a presenter. When I spoke to her again, she said something about only training journalists. What did she mean? I wanted to do her course in order to become a broadcast journalist. I longed to find out how to do things right.

Despite this, she had said, "You can reapply," which was the go-ahead I needed.

After I had received permission to reapply, my preparations for the second attempt began in earnest. I started to buy newspapers, and when my reader came, we would go through them. I paid more attention to the news on both radio and television. I even went as far as to identify stories I could talk about. I completed and submitted an application form.

The response was swift. The university granted me a second interview. By the time it came round to attending it, I felt exhausted. I had put so much effort into preparing for it.

March 2007

I set out in plenty of time to get to the university. In order to get to WMU, I had to catch two buses. The first bus was fine because I used this service all of the time. The second bus was a service that I had used in the past, but only to go in the opposite direction. I knew that when I got on the bus, I would have to ask the driver to let me know when I should get off. I boarded, and was having a word with the driver, when a passenger insisted that she knew where I was going, and that she would let me know when to alight. I sat down. There was no point being rude to this woman by refusing her help.

The journey was scheduled to take about thirty minutes. An island was an indicator that I was approaching my stop. Time went by, and I was beginning to feel anxious. The last thing I wanted was to miss Silver Tree Road. I showed signs of concern. I was reassured that we hadn't reached my stop. Suddenly, somebody told me that we had.

It's a very funny thing, but you know almost instinctively when you've got off at the wrong stop. I wasn't where I should have been, but what could I do about it? This woman was escorting me to... I couldn't say where. We weren't anywhere near the place I wanted.

We seemed to be doing an awful lot of walking. It was clear that this woman had no idea of where I had to get to. She probably didn't even know where she was going to herself. She would have abandoned me if she could. Fortunately, somebody who knew where the university was, helped me to get there.

At WMU, I was late. The interview process had already started.

When it was my turn to be grilled, I answered the questions as well as I could. Having been warned not to talk about wanting to be a presenter, I wasn't sure what to say when Linda Hunt asked me what I wanted to do. I said something about wanting to be a producer. She asked me about the programme I was presenting, but when I told her about it, she wasn't impressed. Nobody had indicated the sort of show I should broadcast. The choice had been left entirely up to me. When this part of the interview was over, we had to do the current affairs test. Once again, I found myself having to dictate the answers to Linda Hunt. Doing so was just as difficult as it had been in the previous year.

However, I felt sure that, when I got to the theory questions, I would be fine. I had prepared three good answers. When the time came for me to do it, Linda Hunt imposed a time frame. This wasn't a part of the question, but she said, "You must write about stories that have happened in the past week." The accounts I had prepared hadn't occurred in the last week. They had all taken place within the past month. I couldn't think of any stories from the last week to use. Then I remembered an account that my reader and I had been talking about only the day before. What I wrote was adequate. The second story I wrote about was one that I had planned. This was an incident I could use because it was an ongoing foreign story. What

The Unfulfilled Promise

I wrote for the third account, I cannot remember. The time was up. I had done as well as I possibly could. The test was over.

After this, I read the news bulletin. For some unknown reason, this was a part of the day I never did well in. Although the university had arranged for the news report to be put into Braille, I didn't like the way it had been done. In Braille, there are no capital letters – that is, not in the UK. However, if a writer wants to indicate that a capital letter has been used, he or she can do so. This involves Brailing an additional character (dot) in front of the letter that is capitalised. From a reader's point of view, this makes the page more crowded and, therefore, more difficult to read. This was what I found when I came to peruse the bulletin. Also, the news report was laid out funnily on the page. Having said that, I had submitted a recording of a well- read article, with my application form; this would have counted for something. The morning was over, thank goodness. After eating a tasteless sandwich, we went back for the afternoon session.

There was one more test to do – headlines. We had to put a list of headlines in order, depending on the audience we were targeting. None of us got the order right, but I suspected that this was the sort of thing that would come with practice. The day was virtually over. All we had to do was to go home and wait for the result. Before I left the building, I heard Linda Hunt make a curious comment, "Somebody will have a job before the course begins."

Two days later, the outcome arrived. It wasn't good news. Linda Hunt did not offer an explanation in her letter, but I knew that, at the first opportunity that came my way, I would phone her to find out why she didn't give me a place. I had done what she had told me to do, but this had not been good enough. According to Norma, "It was because you didn't speak to somebody," who she did not name. I can only presume that my sister must have been referring to The Child. Nobody had ever given me an order to speak to anyone; otherwise, I would have done so. Later, when I spoke to her again, she claimed that Linda Hunt didn't give me a place because I wanted to be a presenter, even though I had not said so. And later still she said, "Linda Hunt doesn't want you on her course." Somebody else said this as well.

Once the weekend was over, I got in touch with Linda Hunt. She told me why I didn't get a place, but I couldn't understand what she was saying. It was something to do with the news. I wasn't a news person. According to her, I had not talked about the news like the other candidates had done. I was late, so I didn't hear how the other candidates dealt with this question. Nevertheless, when Linda Hunt asked me to talk about a story that I might have heard on the news that day, I did. Somehow, I got it into my head that the story I talked about wasn't hard news. It was the second story in the news bulletin that I heard, yet it hadn't been good enough. She advised me to apply to do a production course, and that I should keep in touch with the people at BNUK Central. In order to facilitate my search for a production course, she gave me the name and number of somebody to contact.

As soon as I replaced the receiver, I telephoned the number she had given to me. But all that I could do was give the woman dealing with my call my name and address. She would let me have the information I wanted as soon as possible. Meanwhile, I found out about a university down south, Eastmouth, so I contacted them. They said, "We'll let you have some information."

With regard to keeping in touch with people at BNUK Central, I discovered that the person who had helped me to get the placement wasn't there. He was on an attachment somewhere. I didn't know who else to speak to; nor did I know what else I could do. Failure was an outcome I had never entertained. This was why I told myself that something was wrong, but I couldn't put my finger on it. What was it? I wrote a letter, challenging the decision that Linda Hunt and her colleague had made.

An idea came to me. I remembered hearing about a university up north, Strepton University, which offered the sort of course I wanted to do. I contacted the university, and the person I spoke to said, "I'll let you have the relevant information."

Why I did this I will never know, but I went to see another clairvoyant. Debbie used an object to carry out her readings. I gave her the ring that I had worn for twenty-eight years. Her first observation was, "You're frustrated. You want to move on, but you can't." She seemed to think that I would do so and do very well as a consequence. She also saw that I was being abused and, as a result, I was being left isolated. She was right there.

My sisters knew something about what was going on but wouldn't say anything. Earlier in the year, I had a dream about Frances, my youngest sister. She had been trying to tell me something, but I couldn't make out what it was. I also dreamed about Stephen. What did it mean? Did it mean anything?

I put it out of my mind and focused my attention on the information I had received from Eastmouth University. The production course didn't seem to be too bad. They were going to hold an open day. It would be a good idea to go and see what it would be like. With regard to the second lot of information I had received from Strepton University, I read it, filled in the form, and held on to it.

When I spoke to Gerald again, something about what he said struck me as odd. Once more, he said, "You've been prevented from getting on to the course at WMU." He believed this could not continue. I had a strange feeling he had been told what Linda Hunt had said about doing a production course. He saw me getting on to a course and working on a piece that I had previously written. He felt this was the right way to go. The following day, I posted an application form to Strepton University. The application was late, but the administrator had said, "You can submit it."

April 2007

A response came to the letter that I had written challenging the decision not to give me a place at WMU. The missive gutted me. The letter set out all the things I had not done in order to become a journalist. It disturbed me. Bearing in mind that I had spoken to Linda Hunt before applying for a place, and that I had taken her guidance on board, this letter did not make sense. Now, she was presenting me with a shopping list of all of the things I had not done. The missive terrified me. This baffled me. Desirous to hear what she had written again, I took the letter to Perfect Matches – the organisation which helps people with disabilities to find work – and got somebody to read it to me.

A new woman had joined the team. Her name was Cheryl. She read the letter, and its content appalled her. It struck her as racist. I wasn't so sure about her conclusion, but she went on to urge me to take the matter to the Commission for Racial Equality. She instructed me to write an objective account of what had happened. I said, "I'll do it," and left.

As soon as I got home, I contacted the Disability Rights Commission, who weren't able to help me at that time. I needed some advice, but where could I get it?

I had arranged to do some shopping with Frances. I needed cartridges for my printer. I tried to discuss the matter with her, but she wasn't interested. Was she in the loop of people who knew something? When I saw her again and told her, "I'm going to see a solicitor," she still wasn't concerned. In fact, she did a most unusual thing: she brought wine and cake to the house. She had never done that before.

What was going on? A few days later, BNUK gave me an idea.

I was listening to the radio when I heard an item about cartridges for printers. What a coincidence! Frances and I had gone to the stationery store for cartridges for my printer. I regarded this as a concurrence and nothing more. There was no way they could have found out that I had bought cartridges for my printer – so I thought.

I found a solicitor who was prepared to look at my case. Over and over again, I asked myself if I was doing the right thing. Always, I concluded that if there was something – some sort of discrimination – I would find out. If not, at least I had tried.

At the solicitor's office, I had to wait. When he emerged, he struck me as a pleasant man. I explained what had taken place and handed him the bundle of papers I had put together, along with a statement that I'd written. He glanced through them, making comments as he did so. He decided he would contact the university to obtain any notes they'd made and any other documentation which might shed light on this matter.

I left his office, wondering what would happen. It was quite a scary thing that I'd done – going to see a solicitor. I had never done anything like that before. I hoped that everything would turn out right.

At the book club that evening, the next month's novel was confirmed – *Never Let Me Go* by Kazuo Ishiguro. Fortunately, I had managed to get hold of a copy of the book and I started to read it the following day. As I was reading it, I had a premonition, a warning that Kiss of Death, one of the presenters on *The Morning News,* was going to deal with my applications to go to university. It was as though I could hear a conversation. Somebody who sounded peevish (The Child) was complaining about someone going to university. It was clear that The Child didn't want this person to go to university. A woman, one of the presenters of *The Customer,* was assuring him that Kiss of Death is dealing with the matter. What did this mean?

At this stage, I didn't know how to interpret the conversation I had heard, but the meaning was to become all too clear. But that wasn't the only thing I heard that week.

Two days later, there seemed to have been a commotion over my references. What was wrong with them? I had asked people who had worked with me over the past few years. One of them was an experienced broadcaster. Linda Hunt had led me to believe that my testimonials were fine. I had asked her if I could use them before submitting the form. Once she had sanctioned their use, I had used the same references for other applications. Now, it seemed that somebody was questioning the validity of my testimonials. Why?

Later, Norma phoned me. She hinted that something untoward was going on with my references. She was insinuating that my testimonials weren't appropriate, and this was why I wasn't making any progress with my applications. These conversations confirmed a suspicion that I had held for a long time - that somebody, other than the institutes that I had sent my applications to, had access to them. This was corroborated by the fact that listeners were referred to as the "audience."

As a part of my application for a place on the course at Strepton University, I had to submit a proposal for a dissertation. It had to be five hundred words long. I referred to listeners and viewers as the "audience," in order to meet this word limit. All of a sudden, Kiss of Death would talk about the "audience".

Along with the proposal, I had to send a photograph with the application. On a programme broadcast by BNUK, somebody was analysing some pictures. Was one of them mine? Or was I being paranoid? One question needed to be asked: how did BNUK know where I was applying to?

I had arranged for somebody at Perfect Matches to help me to complete the form, but when I turned up, she wasn't there. My reader and I worked on it together instead. It could have been someone at Perfect Matches who had told BNUK because, the day after Cheryl had said that she thought the rejection letter was racist, *The Morning News* featured a piece about racism. It could have been Gerald. But why should he say anything then tell me that I was being prevented from getting on to courses? I didn't dwell on the matter. If I was invited to attend an interview at the university, I would do my best, but if not...

Around about this time, Eastmouth University held an open day. I had decided to attend it. On the day I set out to go, I could feel the warmth of the sun on my face. At the station, the train was on time. It was a very long journey, but when I arrived at my destination, people were helpful.

At the university, a young woman had been allocated to be my guide. I was early. While I waited, the young woman offered me refreshments – rolls and wine. After I had finished eating and drinking, I went to see the person running the course I wanted to do. I was the first person to arrive at his stand, but I didn't find him very forthcoming. He didn't try to sell his course at all. In the end, I found myself attached to another group of prospective students interested in the journalism course. The person offering advice on this course was much more approachable, and he took us on a tour of the parts of the university which would be useful to us.

After the tour, I spoke to this man who turned out to be very helpful and kind. But it wasn't his course I wanted to do. What he taught wasn't practical for a blind person to do. He ran a journalism course, which focused on radio, television, and Internet broadcasting. Ultimately, he asked, "Why don't you go to WMU?" For many people, that was the obvious choice. It hurt to say, "I did, but they rejected me." After speaking to this very considerate person, the young woman took me back to the main hall where I had some more refreshments and chatted with some of the students. Their friendliness touched me, but it was time for me to go.

Eventually, I boarded the train and was on my way home. I thought about what I had been told. The journalism instructor had suggested that I could go back to shadow one of the students. It sounded like a good idea, and I would have taken him up on his offer, but it was pretty expensive to travel to this part of the country. I was fortunate in that I had a Railcard, which reduced any fares. But there was another reason why I didn't accept his proposal. I had heard something that sounded interesting, and which I should investigate further.

A group of us was in one of the studios. One of the other potential students doing the tour had definitely been interested in improving her career opportunities. From what she had said, she was working at BNUK. She had talked about other courses she had come across. One of the places she had mentioned was on the list of courses that had eventually arrived from the person who Linda Hunt had put me in touch with. She had said, "The course is great!" The following morning, I contacted the university and asked them for information about their production course.

May 2007

In the midst of all of this, I had signed up to receive broadband but couldn't use it. If I wanted anything from the Internet, I had to get others to access it for me. When I bought the computer, I also paid for some home tuition. I had already received a couple of sessions relating to the word processor; now it was time to have a lesson about the Internet. Out of the blue, I received a phone call from the tutor. He said, "I'm in your area, and I'd like to know if it would be all right for me to come along." I had no choice other than to agree. Who knew when he would next be in Sandbury?

The tutor arrived at about half past six one evening, and he taught me how to send emails and gave me some tips for using the Internet. Also, he went over some of the things he had showed me the last time he had come. Then he was gone. To this day, I don't feel that I had my money's worth of tuition.

During the following weekend, I decided to practise sending emails. I contacted various members of my family, asking them for their email addresses.

Once I had obtained this information, I sent emails out, and I waited for the responses. Some answers came, while others did not. What had I done wrong? With time, I got everything right. But I heard a piece which made me wonder.

On *The Morning News,* Kiss of Death was talking about the etiquette for sending emails. He observed that some people who transmit emails don't check them beforehand. For some unknown reason, I thought about the work I had done at BNUK Central on a computer without speech. Was this what Kiss of Death was alluding to? I dismissed it because I hadn't sent any emails while I was at BNUK Central, but was I wrong? In case anyone thinks I'm being paranoid, the following weekend I had a conversation with Norma, who let something slip.

Sometimes, when I'm speaking to Norma, I get the impression she doesn't know what I'm talking about. It was like this on the Sunday evening when I spoke to her. I wanted to find out whether my suspicion about what was going on was right. I felt sure that if anybody knew anything, it would be her. She got on much better with my sister, Martha, than I did. She didn't understand my opening gambit, but towards the end of a very long conversation, she said, "They're playing around with your psychic ability, and they're waiting for a breakthrough."

She need not have said any more. In fact, I doubted whether she would have said anything further. I had to be grateful for the crumbs she had thrown my way.

So, attempts were being made to try to attract my attention through the radio. What should I do? I sat down and wrote a letter, but I didn't send it. It didn't feel right even though my sister had dropped a hint. I had already acted on my psychic sense once and had never received any responses. Therefore, despatching this letter would be a waste of time. I left it. If there was something going on, if the events that were taking place were about help, I wanted to be told. It didn't seem right that people were acting surreptitiously, yet nobody was prepared to talk openly to me about it. Surely, if people were being called on to act in this underhand way, and I was to benefit from it, why wasn't anybody telling me about it? What was the big idea? It struck me as daft that everybody knew about it except me.

Ten days later, I received information about the course at London University – the course I had learned about during my visit to Eastmouth University. Once again, the college said, "It will be all right for you to apply, despite the fact that your application will be late." The woman who took my call made a comment about references, but that didn't bother me because I knew what I was going to do this time. According to the information about the course, it exceeded my expectations. It seemed to cover everything I'd done over the past ten years - the playwriting and the radio programmes. How incredible!

In view of the criticisms that had been made about the testimonials I had used, I got in touch with the university where I had studied years ago. I didn't know who to approach about a reference because it had been such a long time since I'd been there. Many of the lecturers who had taught me would have moved on by now. The person on the phone read out a list of names, and I recognised a few of them. I contacted one of them, and she said, "I'd be more than happy to write a testimonial for you."

The reference took a long time to come through because the university couldn't find my file. Eventually they did, and my former tutor wrote a testimonial and sent it to me.

I felt pleased and proud of what I was doing. I couldn't believe that I was considering London University. No sooner had I put the application in the post when another letter came. I hadn't forgotten about the application I had submitted to Strepton University, but it wasn't exactly preying on my mind. Once more, a university was granting me an interview. I started the process of getting ready straight away.

Frances read newspapers to me. I paid even more attention to television and radio news, and I even had my hair done.

Normally, I have my hair in plaits – extensions – because I like them. I feel comfortable with my hair that way. On this occasion, Frances talked me into having a different style – the weave. Everyone said, "It looks good." I didn't really like it because there was too much hair around my face. Nevertheless, Frances had done it, and I would have to live with it until my hair needed to be done again. By the time the day arrived to go to the interview, I felt more than prepared.

June 2007

I got ready, and when the appointed time came, I left my house. I reached the station in plenty of time, and when the train pulled in, the person on duty put me on it. At Westhampton, I boarded the train for my northward journey. When I got to Strepton, I took a taxi to the university. After presenting myself at reception, the receptionist accompanied me to the canteen. I had arrived early, as advised in the letter, and found that I had to wait.

As I sat there, I realised there was an aspect of university life that I wouldn't like – communal living. I had got so used to living by myself, in my own little house that it would be a great effort to move. But I would be prepared to do it, in order to get on to a course. It would be worth it, and Strepton wasn't too far away from home. Eventually, somebody came to collect me.

Upstairs, the woman who had picked me up introduced me to the person who was going to be carrying out the interviews, David Brown. He seemed pleasant enough. He led me into a large room where I had to wait. While I did this, I watched the news on the television. No other candidate had arrived. By the time the news had ended, another candidate turned up – a man who was local to the area. Not long after he had come, a young woman, also a local, appeared. Shortly after this, the session began.

David Brown conducted the process very well. He explained what it was that he wanted from us. Like the interview at WMU, this was an open one. All of us were questioned in front of each other. When that was over, David Brown gave us our first test – the current affairs test. The exercise at this university was much easier than the one at WMU. I had over-prepared for it because these questions were related to what was in the news as broadcast on television and radio. I didn't struggle over it. The next exercise was the headlines. Once again, I felt this would come right with practice.

The last test was very different. For this exercise, a woman handed us a bundle of newspapers. We had to find a story and say how we would prepare it for a certain type of programme. Somebody had been allocated to help me to read through the newspapers. Not long after going through the papers, we all came up with stories and said how we would handle them. We all did very well. I had never done anything like that before, and I looked forward to doing it again. The meeting was almost concluded when we learned why we had been invited to attend it.

The Unfulfilled Promise

There is a widely held belief that these courses are very difficult to get on to because they are so competitive. Yet we learned that we had been interviewed because the course had not been filled. On that cheery note, we left. I cannot recall what my thoughts were as I travelled home, except to wonder how David Brown had known that I had applied to WMU. Naturally, I wanted to believe I would get through. The following week seemed to go on forever. When I told Frances that I hadn't received a result, she could not conceal her dismay. But that wasn't my fault. However, I will never forget the day when the letter arrived announcing the outcome.

I had a dream that I was to have over and over again. It was of a woman standing in a window. The woman made me think of one of the women who presented *The Morning News*. At the time, I didn't understand its significance – I still don't – but I associated it with disappointments to come.

I was in the middle of preparing my programme for the radio show, when the post came. There was a letter. I had no idea where it had come from. I felt that I ought to find out. There was no one around who could read it for me. If I wanted, I could go into Birmingham and get it read there. It would take forty minutes to get into town, but once I was there, I could go to the library where I could use the scanner to read it.

The reading machine at the library was so easy to use. It was like a photocopier. The person who wanted something to be read had to place the document on the machine's flat surface, pull down the lid, and press a button. This would prompt the machine to scan the literature. After a few seconds, it would start to read the document. It was as simple as that, and the user was guaranteed privacy, provided that he or she wore headphones. The only drawback was that the machine couldn't read all types of print.

I put the letter on the flat surface, pulled down the lid, and pressed the scan button. According to this letter, I had not gained a place on the course at Strepton University. Sadly, the correspondence did not explain why. The letter even went on to say that I couldn't receive any feedback. I would have liked feedback for that interview because I thought I had done very well. As I travelled home on the bus, I thought about the premonition I'd suffered. Later, I would learn something that would explain this experience.

In the meantime, as soon as I got home, I made a terrible discovery. I had left my keys at the library. It would take a long time to go back and pick them up, but I had no option. I wanted to make a phone call to cancel a shopping trip that I had arranged, but I couldn't get into the house. I turned back the way I had come, and jumped on the next bus going into town.

Around about this time, I heard an item on *The Morning News* that constituted bad taste. It was a repetition of a piece which had been broadcast before, but this time, it was done with more gusto. The presenter and guest were highly amused with what they were doing. What did they think the result would be?

Approximately three years earlier, The Child had tried to humiliate me by letting those people who knew me know that I had failed a test. Three years later, Kiss of Death was trying to do it again. I had no doubt in my mind that this item was aimed at me. Again, what did they expect the outcome would be? Was this designed to persuade me to contact them? Or was the purpose to degrade me? Whatever the reason was, there was no way I would respond.

As I lay in my bed that night, I thought I heard someone say, "She was right." What she was saying I was correct about was that there had been an attempt to blackmail me in the past. Therefore, this second attempt was foolish and a wasted effort.

While all this activity was going on, I was still doing my radio programme at Wall Heath Hospital Radio. Even though I had not gained a place at WMU, Stephen and I had decided to continue to do the shows because it would look as though I wasn't interested if I stopped doing them. Although I didn't like the letter I had received from Linda Hunt, which set out a list of things I had not done, one of the tasks she mentioned was something that I had intended to do but had not got round to doing it.

The missive pointed out that I had not done any interviews. My problem was that I didn't have the right equipment. I spoke to the manager of Wall Heath Hospital Radio, who said, "There's recording equipment available that you can use. I'll leave it in the cupboard." The first time we looked in the cupboard, it wasn't there. When we looked again, it was there, so we picked it up. The question that I had to ask myself now was who was I going to quiz? I had an idea, but preparing for it was slow work.

I wasn't adept at using the Internet, even though I had received a tutorial, which should have helped me. I had to go to the library. The librarians found a lot of the information that I went on to use. Before I could use it, it had to be transcribed into Braille. When the information came back from being transcribed, I had to decide whether I could get an interview out of it. I could, and I immediately set about writing some questions. When I had done this, I got in touch with the organisation I wanted to speak to – Wall Heath Football Club.

When I contacted the club, the person I spoke to gave me the name and telephone number of the club's historian. I got in touch with him, and he was more than willing to be interviewed. We agreed on a day and a time, and when I explained that I had a sight problem, he said, "I'll meet you at the bus stop." It was all but done. I was about to carry out my first inquiry for my radio programme. I couldn't wait. On the day in question, it did nothing but rain. I got drenched walking to the railway station. It reminded me of the time when I had set out to catch a train – I was going out for a meal – and the heavens opened. On that occasion, I arrived at the station so wet that one of the staff offered me his jacket. When

I had got to the place where I wanted to be, a woman tried to dry my cardigan out by putting it under the hand drier in the ladies.

Somehow, the tip of my cane got run over and came off. I began to panic. A passerby saw what had happened, rescued the tip, and screwed it back on. I could not thank the person enough. I really thought I wouldn't get to the station on time, but I did. And I didn't have to wait long for the train to come in.

In order to get to where the historian lived, I had to go to Westhampton railway station. Once I was there, I had to get a bus from the bus station. I did not have any difficulties locating the stand I wanted because somebody gave me a helping hand. The bus arrived on time, and when I got to my stop, the driver told me to get off. It was all going remarkably well.

At the bus shelter, I had to wait for the historian to pick me up. He seemed to be taking a long time, and I was beginning to worry. I pulled my mobile phone out of my bag. I was on the verge of ringing him when I realised he was probably on his way. I was right because, not long after this, a car pulled up and somebody said, "Hello." We made our introductions, and I climbed into his car.

At Mr Lawson's house, he led me into the sitting room where a dog greeted us. It transpired that this dog had been abandoned and Mrs Lawson had taken it in. She suspected that it had been ill-treated because, at first, it was nervous. Now, she wouldn't be without it.

After sitting down, Mrs Lawson offered me coffee and biscuits. I appreciated the gesture. However, I couldn't partake in the refreshments in the end because I was doing the interview. The examination was thorough and it lasted approximately forty minutes. Mr Lawson answered my questions very well. The investigation was better structured than I had thought it was.

Basically, I started at the beginning when Wall Heath Football Club was first established, and worked through to the end, looking at how the club was doing today. I cannot say how chuffed I was with the interview and couldn't wait to hear it. Before I left, I checked that it had come out. It had. The tape recorder I'd borrowed wasn't user-friendly. It would definitely take me some time to get used to it. It was time to leave. The historian and his wife took me to Westhampton railway station. I thanked them for their support, and then I boarded my train.

At home, I whipped the tape recorder out of my bag and set about listening to the inquiry. I congratulated myself over it. I stuttered a little bit when asking some of the questions, but it was my first radio interview. I would improve with time. I gave the tape and tape recorder to Stephen to burn onto a CD, in preparation for using it in the programme.

We broadcast the discussion, and it sounded great! We broadcast it in sections. I really liked what I had done, and so did Stephen.

I decided to address another of the criticisms in Linda Hunt's letter. She had censured me for not visiting a newsroom. With this rebuke in mind, I was determined to frequent one. I thought it would be a good idea to approach the person who had helped me at BNUK Central when I had done my placement. Not being very good at sending emails, I asked my reader to assist me.

This caused an almighty row. My reader couldn't understand why I wanted to visit a newsroom, "I've got an application outstanding, and this is something that I've been criticised for not doing." But she was telling me that I couldn't ask to go to a newsroom on these grounds. I certainly couldn't frequent one for the fun of it. This was what she was clearly suggesting. As I understood it, newsrooms are busy places, and the staff wouldn't want people hanging around for the sake of it. According to her, "Going there isn't a good idea." For some reason, known only to her, she didn't want me to go.

We found a compromise. We came across information about an independent radio station's newsroom. I could visit that one.

I wasn't sure whether to phone the station in question. Revealing that I had a sight problem could make things more difficult. Indeed, things did get a little bit tricky, but in the end, I managed to persuade the news editor to let me drop by. I said something to the effect that I only wanted to see how it functioned. I didn't want to be there for a long time. One day would satisfy my needs. He agreed to let me come into his station, and we settled on a date. He also gave me directions as to how to get there, but they were for if I was coming from the opposite way. I would have to make my own inquiries about how to get there, and I did.

When I told my reader that I had succeeded in talking the news editor into allowing me to visit his newsroom, she seemed surprised. I questioned why.

In fact, around about this time, I began to wonder about her. Was she being loyal? During the course of the argument about the newsroom, she had asserted that she was on my side. Who else's side was there to be on? I noticed she would come late. Was she thinking of leaving? Only time would tell, but every Wednesday evening after she had gone, my ears would burn. Was it a coincidence or not?

A week later, I abandoned my usual Friday-morning routine in order to visit Gloss FM. The bus journey was fine. When I got off the bus, I did what Travel Line had told me to do. As I was walking back in the direction the bus had come, a man asked me if I needed any help. I explained where I wanted to go, and he took me there. He put me in the lift, and I got out on the floor where the station was. I met somebody from the station who introduced me to the news editor, Paul Collins.

The Unfulfilled Promise

Paul came across as being a very cheerful man. He led me into the newsroom, which struck me as a large room with desks around the edges. I was seated by a relatively young man, who was operating everything. He told me about his job and what he was doing as he did it. He was a very able person, and it was evident that he enjoyed his work. He reminded me of a captain at the helm of a ship – certain and confident. He converted information into news stories, which became bulletins, and then he would go off and broadcast them. He gave instructions to others, and sympathised when one of them did not have the information he wanted. He talked about other places he had worked at with a mixture of pleasure and pain. I felt privileged to have met him, and to have spent most of the morning with him.

The newsroom itself was pretty quiet. I had been led to believe they were busy places – a health hazard for those who can't see. I met a reporter who was on her way out to cover a story about the early release of prisoners. She seemed friendly enough.

Another reporter turned up later. This time it was a man, but I didn't speak to him. When the young person who I had passed the morning with went to lunch, I sat with another of his colleagues, Rachel, until it was time to go.

The newsroom was one of those places where I could have stayed. Nobody would have troubled me. I could just get on with my work. I told my reader about my visit, but she dismissed it because according to her, "It wasn't a real experience." Okay, it wasn't a genuine experience in the sense that Paul Collins had sent me out on an assignment, but it was a real experience in terms of the insight I had gained about the workings of a newsroom. The letter I had received didn't say I had to do work in a newsroom. It said that I hadn't approached an editor with an original idea. How would Linda Hunt have known that I had written to an editor?

In view of the fact that I had taken the trouble to go to a newsroom, I saw no reason why I shouldn't add this information to the application I had sent to London University. I contacted the university to see if it would be all right to do so. The person who dealt with my query said, "You can because your application has not been passed on to the appropriate people."

When I spoke to Gerald again, I had no doubt in my mind that he had had a conversation with somebody at BNUK about me. In fact, I always believed he'd discussed my situation with someone. He seemed to think that the application to London University should be successful. He said, "You'll be interviewed by a panel of three – two of whom will be on your side. The third you will have to persuade." It all sounded very positive, and I began to get my hopes up in spite of any difficulties.

One of the problems with going to London was that I would have to decide where to live and how to get there. I thought I could travel back and forth, as the course would only require me to go in twice a week. But that would depend on whereabouts in London the university was located. The reality was, I could only answer questions like this when I had received an offer of a place.

Once more, Gerald talked about work. He appeared to think that I should be considering seeking employment instead of wanting to go to university. I pointed out that the reason why I wanted to go to university was because I had applied for several jobs before and hadn't got any of them. He said, "You've gained some experience now." He did not convince me. I must have mentioned the letter.

According to the missive, I had no experience worth speaking about. But Gerald seemed to think that the letter had been sent for a different purpose – forcing me to make contact. Contact with whom? The Child? If this was the case, then once again, it constituted bad taste. What he was saying chimed in with my suspicion that Linda Hunt had not written the missive on her own.

According to the letter, Linda Hunt seemed to think that I had not taken her advice on board. How would she have known that? At the time when she had written her missive, I was waiting for information to come through about the sort of course she had said that I should do. Whatever this experience was about, I was getting weary of it. It was in this exhausted state of mind that I went to see the counsellor.

July 2007

The counsellor appeared to have two concerns on his mind: if I wanted to get into the broadcasting industry, I would have to contact somebody who I knew. He asked, "Are you acquainted with anybody in the media?" I told him that I knew the person who had helped me at BNUK Central, but that wasn't what he wanted to hear. Then he homed in on his second theme, which was about work.

My problem was I didn't know what sort of a job I wanted to do. The counsellor explained the way he advises people to find a position. Somehow, I didn't find his counsel reassuring. His guidance was about making contact with companies, so that when a vacancy came up, my name would be at the top of any supposed list.

He definitely didn't like the college idea. He thought my desire to go to university was wrong. According to him, "You're doing the opposite to what most people do." I didn't go to the trouble to explain that I had applied for several jobs in the broadcast industry before and had got nowhere. I very much doubted whether I would get anywhere now, even though I had some experience under my belt.

On leaving, I felt he had tried his best to dissuade me from wanting to go to university. In fact, he made a comment about university – about getting there – which made me wonder who he'd been talking to about me. Perhaps, more to the point, who had Gerald been speaking to? It was clear that the counsellor had been talking to somebody about my situation because, as I lay in my bed that night, I had a preternatural feeling – a feeling that he had recorded the consultation. He had charged me sixty-five pounds for it.

And the counsellor would have recorded the consultation, because, like Gerald, he looked to BNUK for a commission. In keeping with the counsellor's theme, on *The Morning News* the following day, the presenter, who was a woman, did nothing but go on about how it is better for people with schizophrenia to work. I had no doubt in my mind that she was referring to me. The only problem was, I wasn't, and never have been, schizophrenic.

There had been so many instances when I had heard these people talking about mental illness, and on many occasions, I was certain that these comments were aimed at me because of the sensations I experienced. Evidently, it never occurred to them to ask themselves, if I was mentally ill, what did trying to exploit me make them? In targeting me in this negative way, were they really hoping that I would respond?

The only problem was this: nobody said that I had to reply. As a listener, I knew I could respond if I wanted to, but if that was what they expected from me, they should have made it clear. If they wanted me to react to an attack such as this, what sort of a reply were they expecting? Calling someone something that that person is not would not elicit a polite response, but they couldn't see that. Why were they doing it? It was happening for a reason.

Despite the fact that I knew so many people who were aware of what was going on, nobody was prepared to say anything outright. How daft. Perhaps forthrightness had been forbidden – by The Child or Kiss of Death. I was certain that both of these men were behind whatever was going on.

Having no doubt in my mind that the counsellor had recorded the consultation, I wrote to him saying, "I suspect that our meeting was not treated in a confidential way." I felt his displeasure.

Around about this time, I contacted DHDA. I don't know why I did it, but Samuel was absolutely surprised that I wasn't working. His assertion shocked me so much that I didn't ask him what he meant. It was obvious he had been led to believe I would get work. Where? Doing what? And with whom? How strange it was that Samuel should know something like this and not me. Did this mean that when I had called on him fifteen months earlier, he knew something? Was this the job Norma was talking about when she had a go at me for not sending emails?

She seemed to think that I should be despatching emails, but she couldn't say to whom I should be transmitting them. It was an odd row, and once again, I felt she was withholding something. Why? What was it? What purpose would be served by behaving in this way? It struck me as childish. Were these comments meaningful: the remark that Linda Hunt had made at the end of the interview; Samuel's amazement at the fact that I was not working, and the hints that Norma had dropped – that there was a job for me? Who could say? Nobody.

August 2007

I received a strange communication. It was a recording of a reading from Raymond that I did not request. I hadn't seen Raymond since Christmas. Somebody must have got in touch with him and asked him to do a recording of a reading. Whoever it was had no idea how I interpret these. As I have already said, they are not things that you live by or dwell on. If they come true, they come true. Readings, if they are done properly, are much more sophisticated than people might think. A clairvoyant will indicate how his or her reading will come to pass. He will say, for example, "You will hear about a job." If you are the subject of the reading, you have no idea how this is going to come about, but you certainly don't go looking for one. With the passage of time, you will become aware of a situation, either through a comment that somebody may make, via a message, or through a written form of communication. Shaun had once said that I would learn about a job. I did not know how this would occur, but it did. My reader had left a message on my answering machine, saying that there was a traineeship going at such and such a place.

According to the reading that Raymond now sent, "You should look out for everyday opportunities." He did not give me any indication about what I should keep my eyes open for. My view is that an opening is not an everyday incident. It is a prospect that stands out and which you cannot resist – a carpe diem moment, if you like. This was what had happened two years ago.

I had heard about a writing opportunity for a soap opera. After establishing that somebody would be prepared to help me to find out more about it, I decided to go for it. I went for it with a passion. Nothing was too much trouble, but I didn't get it. Nevertheless, I had seen it as an opening that I could not miss.

The reading went on to apologise for what had happened. I didn't like the reading, and I didn't know what to make of it. It was as though Raymond was talking to somebody about me behind my back because it was in the third person. It never crossed my mind to ask him about it. I just saw it as somebody playing around with something he should have treated with more respect. Looking back, I wonder if there had been a threat in the reading, to the effect that, if I didn't do...

For my part, this experience was about the instruction I had not received, never mind the implied threat.

The Unfulfilled Promise

I had been on the Internet for several months, but I still couldn't use it properly. I found out about an organisation which could give tuition over the phone. This meant I would need a telephone by the computer. I asked Frances if she would help me to get one.

On a bright Saturday morning, we set out to buy a new telephone. We went to a store, which wasn't too far away, and I picked a set of phones that I liked. Before I knew it, I was changing my telephone and broadband provider in order to get what seemed like a cheaper and better deal. What the company was offering sounded too good to be true and I said so at the time.

The following day, I realised what I had done. Somehow, I wasn't happy with the arrangement I had entered into, but I couldn't find the contract to get out of it. I searched high and low for it. After a few days, I contacted the company and cancelled the agreement.

A week after making this purchase, I was listening to *The Customer*, when I heard an item which made me wonder about Frances. Was she telling people at BNUK that she helped me to do this task or another? I had dismissed the business over the cartridges because there was no way she would have contacted them, but more to the point, why should she? Now, I heard a piece about communication packages. It wasn't what the presenter said about them that shocked me. It was hearing the very words that I had used being repeated – "It's too good to be true" – that stunned me. What was going on? Was this a broadcast I should have responded to? What would I have asked: "Has my sister been speaking to you?" It would all have been denied, and I would have been left looking like an idiot – end of contact. Rather than work myself up into a lather, I did what I usually did on a Friday – I went to the gym.

Meanwhile, Stephen and I were still doing the radio programmes. I had done another interview. I questioned the curator of the Lock Museum. The truth of the matter was, I did not know there was a Lock Museum in the area until the manager of Wall Heath Hospital

Radio mentioned it. When I got in touch with the museum, the curator was more than happy to be interviewed. In the end, I was amused by what had happened on my way to this museum.

I had got to Westhampton without any difficulties. From there, I needed to get a bus to where the museum was. When I got on the bus, I asked the driver to put me off outside the Lock Museum. He said, "Of course, I will." When I thought we were approaching the stop I wanted, I reminded him that I needed to be told when to alight. He said, "You've missed your stop." He advised me to get off the bus, cross over the road, and get a bus back to the stop I wanted. I did as he suggested and waited for another bus to take me to the stop where I should have alighted. A bus came, and I boarded it, asking the driver as I did so to let me know when I was at the Lock Museum. He said, "I'll let you know." He forgot. Like the first driver, he advised me to get off the bus, cross over the road, and get the bus on the other side. I did as he suggested. Eventually, another bus arrived, and I got on it and asked the driver to put me off outside the Lock Museum. This driver did not forget. In fact, the bus did not pull away until I was outside the museum, which was not far away from the stop where I got off.

Outside the museum, I waited. For some unknown reason, I thought the curator would be meeting me here. After about five minutes, it occurred to me that I ought to ring the doorbell. I did, and it worked because the door was answered almost immediately. The curator led me through a courtyard and into a strange-feeling room where she gave me a seat. She offered me coffee, and I thanked her for it. But once again, I found I couldn't drink it while holding the tape recorder and interviewing somebody at the same time.

The curator was a young woman who had a pleasant-sounding voice. She answered my questions fully, and when we finished talking about the lock industry – its rise and fall, working practices, and the role of children – we discussed other social issues that would have existed around about the time the lock industry flourished. When I completed the examination, I checked that the recording came out. It did, and it sounded good. It was the first time that I used this digital recorder since acquiring it. As soon as I could, I handed the tape recorder over to Stephen, who downloaded the interview onto a CD. When it was broadcast, it sounded brilliant – much better than the first one. Now, I was on the lookout for another subject to inquire into.

My nephew, Patrick, phoned me. He wanted to know if it would be all right to hold a party at my house to celebrate my birthday with his daughter's. I had let him down when I had not lent him any money to buy a flat. This time, I agreed to his proposal. Neither his daughter, nor I, were celebrating significant birthdays. It was just that his daughter's birthday fell on the same day as mine.

September 2007

When I spoke to Gerald, he suggested that I should write an article. He believed this would lead to employment. No doubt, this was the work that everybody seemed to think I should be doing. Only nobody could say of what it would consist. He hinted that it wouldn't be a job in radio, or at least among the people associated with this affair. That suited me fine.

He went on to say, "Once you've accomplished this – the writing of the article – there could be work abroad." This was an interesting idea because I had spent the past two months preparing a piece about a health condition. Before I did that, I had to inquire about places at London University. I had not heard from them. I didn't know what to make of it. The following morning, I got in touch with them and the woman who responded to my call said, "We'll let you know."

A few days after I had spoken to a woman at London University, I had the dream once again of a woman in a window — one of the women who presented *The Morning News*. This was followed by a letter from London University saying, "We will not be offering you a place." Like Strepton University, they did not explain why they had rejected me. I noticed one thing: The Child was presenting *The Customer* immediately after I had received this letter. Was this a part of the plan? Kiss of Death would block, and The Child would present himself as the helping hand. It sounds awful, but this is how it appeared to me. One thing was certain: if the course had been blocked, what did this mean for the article? I began to panic. Something had to be done, but what? It occurred to me that I should write a note, but I didn't have the courage to do so. What would I say? Would they reply? I put the idea on hold because I came across another idea for an interview.

Purely by chance, my reader and I discovered the Pen Room. I had no idea that such a place existed. My reader downloaded the information about the museum, and after reading it, I contacted the Pen Room. The gentleman who took my call was very helpful. His name was Martin Head. He was one of the people who had had a hand in setting up the museum several years earlier. When I explained what I wanted, he could not have been more supportive. He told me a bit about the Pen Room and how I could get there. He even went as far as to ask, "Do you have difficulties with walking?" I hadn't said anything about my disability. This was an odd question to ask. Or was it? We settled on a date for our meeting.

Two days later, I set out for the Pen Museum. I decided to go on the train. I caught the train from my local station, got off at the next stop, and caught another train to the area where the Pen Room was. At the station near the Pen Museum, a member of the railway staff was waiting to meet me. It was a very deep station, almost like the underground. The number of steps that I had to climb to get to ground level amazed me. Once I was outside the station, it wasn't too far to walk. In fact, I overshot the museum but not by a great distance.

Inside I was in a large room, which was very noisy because of the number of people coming in and out of the building. Every time somebody opened the door, it made a dreadful buzzing sound. It wasn't possible to carry on with the interview in this room, so we moved into another. The second room was just as noisy because a group of people was watching a video about the museum, which was quite loud.

Nevertheless, we persisted, and eventually, we concluded the session. It was a fascinating interview, and Martin was the right person to talk to. He had so much to say about the rise and fall of the pen industry, working conditions, and the emergence of a union to represent workers in this industry.

When I had finished speaking to Martin, I looked at some of the artefacts that the museum held. I saw old typewriters, a stenographer's writing machine, and a Braille shorthand machine. I would not have expected to see something like that displayed in a Pen Museum - but it was because it had been designed by somebody who lived in the area. Seeing it took me back.

When I had left school in 1975, I went to a college for the blind in Shropshire. It was eight miles from the nearest town, and one mile from the local pub. To get into the nearest town, the college laid on a coach on a Friday afternoon and a Saturday morning. There was a bus, but it only ran once a week – on a Wednesday. As for getting to the pub, we walked to it, which was lovely in the summer. It was at this pub where I tried to smoke for the first and last time, and I didn't like it. The college grounds were beautiful. In the centre was a huge lawn.

At the north side there was the castle. This building was full of rooms, many of which we didn't go into. Some of the floors were uneven and creaked. In here, we ate our meals. They weren't too bad. The castle also housed the offices and the staff common room, and it was where some of our lessons took place.

On the east side of the lawn stood the halls of residence. The women's block was a modern affair, whereas the men's building used to be an old stable block. I never ventured into the latter, so I couldn't say what it was like inside. To be honest, men and women weren't allowed to go into each other's buildings.

On the west side of the lawn there were trees, and at the south-westerly point was the driveway, along which was the swimming pool. The college expected us to go swimming. I went for a few lessons but soon stopped. I didn't like it. My problem was I was finding it difficult to get over an experience that I went through when I was at school.

I was swimming one day when something happened. I didn't know what it was, but I believed I was going to drown. To make matters worse, the PE teacher just stood on the side and did nothing to help me.

From the south-east point there was a path which led to the woods. And at the south side, there were more trees.

The north-west corner of the lawn pointed to another pathway which led to the gardens. They were beautiful. One summer, we helped to pick fruit. We enjoyed ourselves.

At the north-east point of the lawn was a path which led down some steps into the vicinity of the shack. The shack was a low-level building where our typing lessons took place. These were not exciting. Term by term we worked on our typing skills, and as we progressed, our tutor entered us for various typing exams. Shorthand was much more thrilling.

The Unfulfilled Promise

The Braille shorthand system was immensely complicated. There was far too much to take on board. In the end, I learned as much as I thought I needed to know. I could write at a speed of one hundred and twenty words per minute.

Writing at speed was fun. One of the teachers who taught us would always commence with, "Are you ready? Then we'll begin." She read with her nose pressed against the page, and her voice was high, clear and well pronounced. We pounded away as she dictated, and broke off just a little while after she finished reading.

The other teacher from whom we took dictation was the opposite. To start with, he was Australian. When he read, he upped the speed without us knowing. Quite often he would say, "Shorthand is about memory." He said this because we ceased writing after he stopped dictating. I regarded it as a pity that I never used my shorthand skills as much as I thought I would when I was at work.

Also, in the vicinity of the shack was the library and the bar. The library was a relatively new building, and our English lessons were taught in one of the library's big, comfortable rooms. The group I was in was quite large. We were taught by a highly experienced Welshman.

A limited number of academic subjects was on offer. At the time, I studied the subjects I thought were right.

The bar was not a very big place, but I always felt at home there. In those days, I drank lemonade and blackcurrant. I cannot recall going to the bar with anyone, so I must have gone on my own. Cookery was on the timetable too.

The kitchen, which was in the women's block, was huge. I learned how to use an electric oven. We made a variety of dishes, such as orange soufflé, Bakewell tarts and fatless sponge. Also, we made sausage plait, beef and tomato casserole and cream of chicken.

The tour of the museum was over, and Martin escorted me back to the station, where there was no one around to help me. Martin waited with me until my train pulled in. It seemed to take an age. As I travelled back, I thought about the station and vowed that I would never go there again. It was like a deserted ship – large, deep, and empty. I found myself wondering if my reader had said something to The Child about the fact that I had discovered the Pen Museum. It struck me as odd that Martin had asked me if I had difficulties with walking.

In view of the other suspicions I was beginning to harbour about my reader, I decided to ask her about it. The last thing I wanted was to make a big issue of it. However, I needed to know whether she was betraying me or not. At that time, it didn't occur to me that she might lie about it. Making the inquiry as casual as I possibly could, I asked her if she had said anything to anybody about the Pen Museum. She said, "I have not, and I would not do so because I am a Christian." I had to take her at her word. But since when has being a Christian prevented anyone from lying?

Frances phoned me. She asked me if I wanted to go for a walk on the hills. I said, "I would," and an hour later we were ascending a steep hill. Unusually, I found climbing up the hills hard going. Every now and again, I had to stop. It wasn't because of breathlessness, just an inability to keep going. We carried on walking, sitting on every bench we passed. Eventually, we arrived at the coffee shop, where we stopped off for jam scones and coffee.

A week later, *The Morning News* featured a piece about disadvantaged people accessing the countryside.

October 2007

A postal strike was imminent. Something had to be done about the fears I had. If nothing was said, the article would be blocked. I had no doubt in my mind that this would happen. Using the strike as a deadline, I wrote a note, addressing it, "To whom it may concern." I couldn't leave things as they were. I hoped that any response I received would serve as a guide as to what I should do. After all, that was what I was looking for – advice. Norma, the counsellor, and Samuel had dropped inexplicable hints.

One morning, I wrote a note pointing out that I had sustained a psychic experience in which I had been led to believe, if I made contact, somebody would get in touch with me. I had made the contact – getting on to three phone-ins and sending in numerous comments and notes – but nobody got in touch with me. Yet, everything I was trying to do was being undermined. I begged for guidance. I posted the note. I felt courageous in sending it.

The question was this: did I expect a reply? I waited. What came was a sense of disapproval. Somebody was not happy about receiving that note. Why? Nobody should have known that The Child should have replied to my contacts. This was a very strong feeling that I had. Somebody did phone, but whoever called left no number. Who was it? Was it The Child? I had no way of knowing.

I had an appointment that I wasn't looking forward to. In the summer of this year, I had gone to see my GP. She thought I seemed dejected. I probably was. I never imagined that I would endure so much. I was trying to do something positive with my life, and it was being wrecked, and nobody was saying why. That would have depressed anybody. She persuaded me to speak to the community psychiatric nurse. In the end, I had seen no harm in meeting him.

When the time came, I felt quite nervous, but the nurse turned out to be a pleasant young man. I told him my story. He was sceptical about it: why should BNUK want to concern itself with somebody like you? Precisely. I mentioned that I had spoken to a counsellor about it and gave him the counsellor's name. The nurse suggested that I should take some medicine. I said, "I don't want that." My problem wasn't mental but psychic. I needed to learn how to protect myself.

Ultimately, he recommended that I should speak to a psychiatrist. I agreed. As I left, I asked him not to send any letters to my house. If my reader got sight of such a document, she would pass its contents on. He said, "I won't send any letters to your house." I had forgotten that I had given him the name of the counsellor I used to consult.

I set about writing the proposal for the article that I had in mind. It was going to be about a condition called tropical spasticity paraparesis, a degenerative disorder that affects more women than men and for which there is no cure. In my piece, I would be arguing that screening should be allowed for this condition. I had already interviewed two women with this disorder and had done some research on the condition. My brother-in-law, Larry, a haematologist, had wanted to write a thesis on this subject at one time, so I asked him to look over the article I had written. He re- ordered a list that I had put together and clarified one point. Once he had done this, I posted it. The person to whom I sent the proposal was on leave. I could have let somebody else have it, but I decided to wait until the journalist who normally deals with health matters came back.

On the day this person was due to return to work, I had a strange experience. In my mind's eye, I saw an image of a man on the phone. It struck me that it was Gerald. What did the image mean? I was to learn its significance later, and the information would clarify a lot of things for me.

Meanwhile, I received no response from the journalist to whom I had sent the article. I had a suspicion that my reader had told either the Child or Kiss of Death that Larry had made some changes to it.

Once again, I contacted Gerald. I didn't think he was pleased to hear from me. In the note I had written, I had probably implicated him. Not only had he always said that I had been prevented from getting on to courses, he had also said that they couldn't keep on stopping me. Comments such as these weren't always said as part of a reading. Now, he was advocating that submitting a play to a small theatre company might be a way forward. I really didn't know what to make of this, but a few days later I received a newsletter from Dramatique, informing me that a small theatre company was looking for one-act plays. His prediction had come true. Or had it?

When my play had been rejected two years earlier, I had asked for a critique on it. I sought the report out. After reading it again, I started the task of making improvements to the play. The first thing that was wrong was the title. I changed it from *An Uncle Calls* to *Uncle Leavy's Visit*. The person who had criticised the play seemed to think that I was trying to write my own version of *An Inspector Calls*. Then I went through the script contracting the speech, and the last thing I changed was the ending. I made it less predictable. Once I had done that, I asked my reader to reformat it. Originally, I had word-processed it on a dos-based computer. When I opened it in a Word document, it was thrown out of line.

I wouldn't say this was a fun task to perform, but when you knew what you were doing, it wasn't so bad. I'm sure it wasn't the job she was doing that made her behave in the way she did, but whatever it was, I found her manner hurtful and offensive.

She was scathing in her rebuke of the play. That had not been her attitude when she had worked on it two years ago. I got the impression that she had liked it then, but now... What had got into her? Why was she being so critical? Some of the comments she was making weren't justifiable. It was as though she was repeating something she had heard. In fact, her manner was so unlike her – so brutal – that I recognised it. She made me flinch, and the last time that had happened was when I was at DHDA. Tony had said things that made me wince, but I had concluded that they weren't his words. What my reader was saying now weren't her words either. I had no doubt in my mind whose influence she was under.

I contacted Frances. Our conversation was brief. I asked her for her opinion about somebody who slagged another person off. She said, "I would think badly of the person, especially if the slagger didn't know the individual he or she was putting down."

By the end of the week, the play was ready to be despatched.

November 2007

Evidently, someone from BNUK found out where the play had been sent to, because on *The Evening News,* I heard the presenter quote the very last words spoken by the main character, "Doing nothing isn't an option." This shocked and offended me. My work was being passed around like a parcel at a party. As if that wasn't enough, I had to contend with the attitude of my reader.

When she came a couple of days after I had heard this broadcast, she was unable to maintain a good temper. She seemed to think it was her business to tell me how to treat Stephen. It was as though she was saying, "You ought to be grateful for the help that Stephen gives you." She would never know how appreciative I was of his assistance, but I certainly didn't need her to tell me how to think. What had brought this mood on?

I concluded that The Child didn't like the idea of the play being used to help me into the broadcasting industry. By being rude to me, my reader was showing him some sort of solidarity. In other words, all she was demonstrating was how influenced she was by The Child.

The Unfulfilled Promise

The community psychiatric nurse broke his promise. He wrote to me saying, "I've passed your file on to a psychiatrist." My reader saw this letter, and I had no doubt in my mind that she communicated its contents to BNUK. On *The Morning News* the following morning, Kiss of Death talked to somebody about betrayals in political life. This certainly was a betrayal, but what for? Not long after I had received this letter, somebody from the hospital phoned me. The person wanted to make an arrangement for me to see the doctor, and I didn't have long to wait.

At the hospital, the psychiatrist took me into a room. Once we were settled, I told her my story, during which she made copious notes. After a while, she said something that sounded like a warning. She was warning me about Gerald. Apparently, he was betraying me. Through him, Kiss of Death had learned about my intentions and could, therefore, block my progress. In fact, when I thought about it, Gerald himself had indicated that the only way I would succeed was if Kiss of Death didn't know what I was doing. The psychiatrist made me promise not to have anything more to do with Gerald.

Not only did she drop this hint, but she said something else as well. Norma had said a similar thing, which made me wonder whether there was an attempt to cover something up. According to this doctor, "In some cases students may be told what to do, but that wouldn't guarantee them a place on a course." That was what had happened to me. How did she know? The counsellor, of course. So, I concluded that I had been rejected from WMU on account of The Child. She wanted me to have a blood test and make another appointment for the New Year.

At home, I thought about the caution the psychiatrist had given to me. I knew that I would have to write to Gerald. I did, and his reply was one of denial. He said, "BNUK want to split us up." I phoned Consumer Direct. It occurred to me that it couldn't be right that I was paying Gerald for a service, and he was exploiting my situation by telling others, who would use what he said against me. According to Consumer Direct, "This is a matter for the Information Commissioner's Office." The next thing I heard was very disturbing.

On *The Morning News* the following day, I caught a piece about the Information Commissioner's Office. Was this a coincidence? Or wasn't it? Had my phone been hacked? Or did the revelation that I had found out that Gerald had been betraying me prompt somebody to realise the wrong that had been committed?

Something else crossed my mind: the play. Surely, this was in jeopardy. Could I do anything about it? I sent an email to the company asking them not to pay any attention to anyone who tried to interfere with the process.

I was listening to BNUK Central when I heard about an opportunity to make a programme with them and later have it broadcast. I contacted the Pen Room to see if Martin would be interested in being interviewed. He agreed. All that I had to do now was to send in a proposal. I worked out what I had to do in terms of how Dorri wanted the bid and then I submitted it.

Dorri accepted it. The only thing that we had to do now was to fix a date. We hit upon one on which we all agreed, and I set about reviewing the questions I had asked Martin when I had interviewed him earlier in the year. This time, I made sure the questions fell within the structure of the plan that I had sent in. Everything was ready.

On a bright afternoon in November, I went to BNUK Central. It felt great! When I got to reception I had to wait because Dorri, who was in charge, wasn't around. She arrived and introduced herself. She also presented me to the person who was going to be operating the broadcasting desk, Barry. It turned out that he had a bundle of CDs. I didn't know any of them. This baffled me. I was only going

The Unfulfilled Promise

to need three songs for my programme – all of which contained some reference to writing.

Somebody else came. It transpired that the studio had been double-booked. The question was which one of us was going to go first? In view of the fact that Martin had not yet shown up, we couldn't go first, but I said I would like to. No sooner had I said this than Martin arrived.

Before we began the recording, we had to do a voice test. Once Barry had performed this task, I started the interview. It went really well. We discussed the rise and fall of the pen industry, working practices, and the formation of the union, among other things.

Martin talked with authority about his subject. I didn't have to worry about him drying up. I introduced each of the records on my list and carried on with the interview. We used more than our allotted time, but I didn't know whether this time included the music or not. I had done it, and I could not hide my pleasure. Dorri said, "I'll let you know if we're going to broadcast it." The only question was: how long would that take? As we left the building, I mentioned Wall Heath Hospital Radio. Martin seemed surprised that I was still there. Where did he think I was? Was it really the case that he had been spoken to? If so, by whom? And why?

In my mind's eye, I saw a window. It was clear. When I checked my emails, there was one from Dorri, saying, "Your program will be broadcast in a fortnight's time, but that I'll confirm this nearer the time." I was bursting with delight, but when two weeks had gone by, I had still not heard from Dorri.

On the day when the programme was due to be broadcast, Frances asked me if I wanted to go for a stroll. I said, "I would," and within a short space of time after leaving the house, we were on the hills. Yippee! But like before, I could hardly walk. I kept on having to stop for rests. This wasn't like me at all. After completing a circuit, we headed for the coffee shop where, once again, we had jam scones and coffee.

I stayed awake to see if the programme would come on. It did, and it sounded fantastic! At last, something positive had happened!

I was looking for another idea for a radio interview. I hit upon the idea of doing one about Westhampton racecourse, which had been going for years. It should make a good programme. When, however, my reader and I looked on the Internet, the information we found wasn't very useful – not for my purposes. I thought no more about the idea because I knew that another one would come my way, and it did.

As I listened to *The Customer* on the following Monday, I heard a piece about Westhampton racecourse. I couldn't believe it! Had I not been sitting on the floor, I would have collapsed on to it. My reader must have said something to them. This was too much of a coincidence. Besides, I had a powerful negative sensation afterwards. I would have to ask her about it. Once more, the last thing I wanted was to create a scene. Again, she informed me, "As a Christian, I wouldn't betray you." I had to take her word for it. Until I had any evidence – hard proof – there was little I could do.

I had a presentiment. For some unknown reason, I found myself thinking about a new reader. Working with somebody I was not happy about was far from ideal. However, replacing her wouldn't be easy. When, a few hours later she came and finished her work, she handed me an envelope as she was leaving. In it was a letter announcing her intention to resign. According to her, she couldn't work with somebody who didn't trust her. This came as a complete surprise to me. I wrote a statement setting out why I thought she was being dishonest.

The next time she came, I gave her the list, but she denied everything that was on it. I asked her if she thought I was mad. She said no. When I asked her about having a go at me over Stephen, she said, "I can't remember doing it." I tried to give her the opportunity to go, but she wouldn't fall for it. I felt she was getting herself into knots. On the one hand, "I can't work with somebody who doesn't trust me," but on the other, she wasn't prepared to go. What could I do? I had arranged to go shopping with Frances. Preferring to get on with that rather than continuing with this futile argument, we left.

My reader had said, "I'll read for you until the end of the year," and she continued to do so, refusing to accept any payment. It wasn't long before I understood why. It made it easier for her to spy. There were times, however, when I wondered why she came. Her moods were so foul. As long as I live, I will never understand why she did not feel able to drop a hint about the association she was having with BNUK. What had The Child said about me that made her so loyal to him?

She was being used, and the worst of it was, she wouldn't have cared even if she had been told.

December 2007

On *The Customer*, there was an interview with somebody representing the Information Commissioner's Office, which was interesting. An item I had seen on IBN news made me wonder if somebody had approached the psychiatrist. The package on the news seemed to be questioning the ethics of breaching patient confidentiality. As crazy as it sounds, it was something the presenters at BNUK would do. They had no sense of decency, but what was the rationale behind their thinking? I bet there wasn't one, except do it because they could. It didn't matter that I had to see a psychiatrist because of them.

I had the blood test the psychiatrist wanted me to have. The result indicated that I needed to take iron tablets. Not long after going on these, I heard an item on *The Morning News* about supplements, and it was stressed how black people are more likely to suffer with deficiencies as opposed to white people. Was there a link? I thought there was.

For years, I had worn the same ring. One day, it just snapped. Frances agreed to help me to buy a replacement. As it turned out, I bought two – one nine carat and the other eighteen.

Once at home, I tried to find out what she knew about the association people were having with BNUK. All she would say was, "You ought to write a book."

Why was it that no one could say anything when something clearly needed to be stated? I left the matter alone.

My nephew, Patrick, phoned me. He said, "I'll be arriving early tomorrow morning." When he had assured me that I would not be lumbered with the expenditure for the party, I had confirmed that he could hold it at my house. All day, I was on the lookout for Patrick and his girlfriend. I was afraid to go anywhere in case they turned up. At five o'clock they came, transforming my house into bedlam.

Almost immediately, they went shopping and returned with more food than I had seen in a long while. Straight away, they put food in the oven – chicken and lamb – and how lovely it smelled as it was cooking. The phone started to ring. This was ever a sign that Patrick was around. Someone somewhere wanted to get hold of him. When the landline wasn't occupied, his mobile was on the go. He was always in demand. Then, to the surprise of his girlfriend and I, he announced that he had to go out, taking the children with him. Nobody knew where he was going, nor did we know when he would come back. Suddenly, he seemed oblivious to the

The Unfulfilled Promise

fact that more preparations needed to be made for the party he had insisted on. Yet, at the first opportunity he had, he disappeared.

His girlfriend and I rearranged the furniture and waited for the food to cook. When we had done everything that could be done the night before a party, we went to bed. Shortly afterwards, we were woken up by Patrick, who had returned with two sleeping children.

The following morning, Patrick and his girlfriend had to do more shopping. They had to do more cooking as well, and then the guests began to arrive. People we had not seen in years showed up. Soon, they had formed groups, and much chatter and laughter played against a background of music. Amidst this, I heard something.

My nephew was telling Norma that his mother couldn't come to the party because of me. Why? What had I done to prevent her from being here?

I had an idea that I should contact somebody about what was going on. The question was: who could I ask? The following day, I sent an email to Tony, setting out the situation. I hoped he could shed some light on it. I never received a reply, yet... I had a strong feeling that, at around half past five that evening, the Child had been contacted.

2008

January 2008

A new year and a new hope – but what will the year bring?

Whatever this experience that I was going through was about, I didn't like it. I didn't like the feeling that everybody knew something about me that I should have known, but nobody was prepared to say anything about it. No matter how hard I tried to find out, nobody wanted to say what it was they knew. I was being isolated, shut out, and left on my own. Although I live by myself, I have never felt as lonely as I have throughout this experience. Perhaps, the gaps of loneliness was the reason why I went to see so many clairvoyants.

The reading with Angela had an air of unpleasantness about it. For the first time, the company she worked for wanted the money before the reading commenced. Unusually, she proceeded by giving me a warning that these readings were only for guidance. Once again, I thought somebody had tampered with the reading.

The Unfulfilled Promise

The reading started with a card denoting that somebody was trying to rule my life. That was true. Blocking these courses was about control. Even though I had written a note in a bid to find out what was going on, nobody had bothered to answer it. This was indicative of somebody wanting things his own way.

Angela picked out a card that suggested regret. There was a lot to rue – that things had not turned out as I had thought they would. She placed a lot of emphasis on specialist support. I couldn't help but feel that somebody had said something to her about my forthcoming appointment with the psychiatrist. Clairvoyants don't normally get dates right, but she was pretty accurate about the date of my consultation. She seemed to think that something would happen around the time of the appointment. At first, I would be upset by the event, but eventually my life would be transformed by it.

Then she picked up a card relating to trust. Was there someone around me who I couldn't rely on? There was — my reader. It wasn't so much my reader I didn't trust, but the influence she had fallen under. Another card she selected showed that I would receive a lump sum of money from some enjoyable work or compensation.

Angela made a lot of reference to the past, and she seemed to think that I would bring something from my past into my present life. She asked me what I had wanted to do when I was ten. When I was ten, I had wanted a typewriter, among other things. She appeared to be suggesting that I would write something. Not happy with her reading, I went to see someone else. This reading was much better and more professionally conducted. First of all, the clairvoyant told me about numerology. When dates of birth are added together, they can give you an indication of what you should be doing in life. Mine signalled that I should work in the communication field.

After that, he went through when the new and full moons would occur. I had not thought about this. Finally, before the reading began, he explained how important it was to be protected. He advised me to buy a pendant and get it blessed in holy water.

The reading was a good one. Everything really sounded positive – too confident, some might say. Then he came to the part of the reading where he wanted an object.

I was unsure what to give him. I had recently bought new rings but I felt that a good reading would not be possible from them because I had not worn them for long enough. In the end, I gave him my watch. From this, he revealed an extraordinary discovery. He said, "Somebody should have got in touch with you, but he's making up excuses." He asked me if I had any idea who this might be. I told him, hesitantly, "The Child." He referred to the experience as an unfulfilled promise, and he went on to say, "The person concerned is sly, nasty, and underhanded." This wasn't the first time a clairvoyant had spoken unflatteringly about The Child.

The clairvoyant had confirmed that somebody should have got hold of me. Perhaps, this was the reason why, despite everything I heard on the radio, I couldn't make contact. As a consequence of this, I was psychologically blocked and could not have got in touch with him – not in the way I think he may have wanted – even if I was inclined to do so.

At the end of this week, I had a very unusual dream. Someone who I had not seen for a long time was telling me – urging me – to apply for a place at Strepton University. Why? I had no idea what it meant. The following morning, I received a newsletter from Dramatique containing guidelines for writing for radio. Was somebody trying to tell me that my play hadn't been successful? Something had happened to it, of that I was sure. I set about reapplying for a place at Strepton University. I also wrote to WMU to see if it would be all right to reapply there. According to the solicitor, who discovered that I had been denied a place when I had first applied, "It will be all right to reapply."

The Unfulfilled Promise

I was dreading this day. It was the day when I had to visit the psychiatrist. Before I left my house, I heard a couple of features on the radio. One of them reminded me of the article that I had wanted to write about screening. Hearing this piece just confirmed in my mind that BNUK had obtained a copy of the proposal that I had written. After the broadcast, I had a most excruciating ear-burning sensation, as though somebody was disapproving of something.

The next package I caught made me think about the article that I had succeeded in getting published. Perhaps, it was this tiny success that was being rejected. Who knew what it was, but it was time for me to go. At the hospital, I didn't have to wait for too long to see the doctor, and when I saw her, it was a brief consultation. I told her, "I'm on iron tablets, and I can hardly do any exercises at the gym." She said, "That's to be expected."

I told her, "I feel everybody knows something that I should know, and that people pitted me." I had never experienced this before – abject compassion. When I rang my reader to check if she was all right to come, she would invariably express pity. The women at the gym also felt sorry for me. They never used to do this. The psychiatrist asked me about contact with my family – did they visit me? I told her that it didn't work like that. If I wanted help, I would ring, but otherwise, I never heard from anyone except Frances.

I mentioned that I had stopped going to the social club that I used to go to. She asked me an extraordinary question about hidden microphones. Was I aware of them? What was she getting at? Was she recording this consultation? Of course, BNUK had approached her, but why? All they would have done was confirm my story. The psychiatrist asked me whether I had heard anything: had something been said that I shouldn't have been privy to?

What was that about? Eventually, the consultation came to an end, and the doctor discharged me. The thing that should have happened did not. Why? Evidently, whatever it was about, it had not been worth the worry. I let out my breath and left the hospital.

Not long after the appointment, I had a preternatural feeling – an excruciating ear-burning sensation.

It indicated that the psychiatrist had recorded the consultation. Why? Was I never to have any peace and privacy? This sentiment was echoed by the presenter on *The Evening News* programme.

A very rare request was made of me. Toby, my youngest brother, a policeman, wanted me to babysit for his children. I had not done this for a very long time. Why now?

When my nephews came the following evening, I had to keep the youngest one, aged seven, amused. I taught him how to write his name in Braille and how to write it on the computer. When he had finished doing that, he wanted his parents. He pestered me to ring them, but they weren't at home. Meanwhile, his elder brother occupied his time by playing with his Wii. Both of them went to bed without any difficulty. Before they left, I asked them to make sure they had packed everything, but they did not. No sooner had they gone than I found a coat and a pair of jeans.

Later on in the day, Frances visited me. We had a pleasant chat. We got on to talking about what I was trying to do. By this time, I had started to write a book. I told her so and asked her to keep it to herself. As soon as Frances left the house – and she couldn't leave it quickly enough after being told this – she picked up the phone and passed on what I had just told her to her associates at BNUK.

A couple of days later, I heard a piece on *The Morning News* about somebody who had written a book in very unusual circumstances. In the meantime, at the same time, I got my reader to read newspapers preparatory to applying for a course. I had set Frances up. She had been passing information about me on to BNUK. There was a little bit of awkwardness between us after that. She knew and I knew what she had done, but I didn't ask why. What would have been the point?

February 2008

I was about to go to the gym when I heard an item which caught my attention. Someone had written an essay about changing circumstances. I thought this was aimed at me because he gave great emphasis to the fact that during his lifetime, he had kept a "good bank of friends." I had told the psychiatrist that I didn't have any friends. Weeks later, Frances quizzed me about my friends, "What's happened to so and so?" But this wasn't all that I heard.

I was getting ready to go into Birmingham to buy a birthday present for Frances when I caught an item about watches. This stopped me in my tracks. It was a watch that the clairvoyant had used to confirm that The Child should have contacted me. The clairvoyant must have recorded the reading and let certain people listen to it. Why? Was I really expected to respond to this? How brutal.

Because I feared that something had happened to the play, I decided to reapply to WMU. After all, I had taken on board many of the criticisms raised in Linda Hunt's letter. I found somebody who was prepared to help me to fill out the form, and this time, I enclosed a recording of a news bulletin that I had read. At the end of the week, I posted the application form.

It seems, however, that everybody was given access to my application because, according to Toby, "There are new things on your form." How would he have known that? Of course, there would be fresh things on my application; I had addressed most of the strictures that Linda Hunt had made.

After I had sent this application, I also worked on one for Strepton University. I did the exercises accompanying the application – writing a news story and reading a news bulletin. It came out very well. I used my digital recorder to make the recording. When I listened to it, it sounded slow, but once I burned it onto a CD, it sounded fine.

Meanwhile, I was still doing my radio shows. By now, I had added a news bulletin to them. Ideas for interviews were beginning to run dry. Nevertheless, I still enjoyed doing the programme and hoped it would lead somewhere soon.

Over two weeks had elapsed, and I had not heard anything about the application I had submitted to WMU. In the past, I had heard something within a couple of days. I plucked up the courage to ring Linda Hunt. How chilly she sounded. Perhaps she had taken offence because I had gone to a solicitor about her letter. It seems that we have rights, but when we exercise them, nobody likes it. She said, "I'm not dealing with your application, but somebody will be in touch soon." I thanked her and replaced the receiver.

Sometimes things happen, and although we might suspect foul play, we are not always prepared to take it on board because the idea is so horrendous. This happened when I contacted another clairvoyant who wasn't, in my view, very good. Was it really possible that somebody would have gone to the trouble of contacting all the clairvoyants in the area to get them to record their readings with me? This was an idea that was going through my mind. Of course, I didn't want to think it was possible because the idea sounds so ridiculous, but was it?

The clairvoyant I went to see disturbed me. He talked about a situation being poisoned. That was true. He mentioned there were people who wanted me dead. There was certainly plenty of talk about suicide on BNUK. It seemed that, whenever I didn't get something I wanted, I would hear a discussion about suicide. When I hadn't gained a place at WMU last year, there had been a feature on *The Evening News* about suicide. But the substance of what the clairvoyant was saying was awful.

He talked about the law, and that I would be given an opportunity to pursue an action if I was successful. Also, I would be taking action if I wasn't. I wasn't sure what he meant. He hinted at some underhanded practice going on since 2006. He talked about trust or rather the lack of it, and then he mentioned Anna. I couldn't remember who she was at the time of the reading. Later, however, I did recall who she was.

Now, though, I realise that the clairvoyant had not been talking about Anna, but one of the female presenters on *The Morning News*. Anna was the leader of the creative writing course that I'd studied about nine years ago.

I had found out about the course late, and the tutor responsible for students with a disability told me to join the group in Norchester. When I went to Norchester, the tutor said, "The university has agreed that you should go to Birmingham." When I turned up at Birmingham, Anna told me to go to Norchester because the group in Birmingham was too big. The class was large but not for long. I was not fooled.

Anna made it absolutely clear that she didn't want me in her group. Perhaps, this was the reason why I didn't like this woman, who I likened to an iceberg – freezing and jagged with an ability to tear. By way of contrast, the professional writer who taught on the course was much better. Her only fault was to write in an article that we did not "burn" as budding writers. When the student who had seen the criticism drew it to her attention, she sent us a note of apology.

March 2008

A story broke in the news about an MP who had been bugged while visiting a constituent in prison. This highlighted the issue of recording interviews. *The Morning News* seemed to dedicate a whole programme to this issue. They were saying, "Local authorities have got the right to watch anyone they suspect of being involved with terrorist activities." I'm not a terrorist, but my conversations were being recorded. Why?

In fact, the reason why they were treating me in this way came out in the programme: so that they could block my progress. The person to whom this comment was made was not impressed.

I posted the application to Strepton University. Two days afterwards, I had one of the most disturbing dreams of this experience. I was actually presenting a show when a man came into my room.

I stabbed him. In my mind, it was The Child. He had obstructed the play. It was as though the dream was saying that he had cut my lifeline. It symbolised something – loss of reason on The Child's part. What would he have to fear if the play was successful? According to Norma, "Whoever hindered the play did so because the competition was very fierce." So why bar it? If it was hopeless, it would fail. Perhaps The Child was not prepared to take that risk.

The following morning, I received yet another newsletter from Dramatique setting out guidelines for writing for radio.

Around about this time, I also had an unpleasant dream about my reader. She was having an argument with her mother. The dream was telling me she was being disloyal.

Forty-eight hours later, my reader's mother phoned me. She asked, "Are you alright?"

WMU granted me another interview. How wonderful. Straight away, I set to work preparing for it. I made arrangements with the woman who used to help me at the supermarket to read newspapers to me. I thought of ideas I could talk about as a story. I had quite a few of them.

The interview was unlike the other ones I had attended in that I was on my own and I was questioned by two different people. It seemed they weren't interested in why I wanted to do the course. Their attitude annoyed me very much. Once out of this sticky situation, I felt that I recovered myself pretty well. Then it came to dealing with the story, and all the ideas I had thought about went out of my head. I tried to recall something I had heard about post offices because it had triggered an idea, but what I thought wouldn't come. In the end, I talked about the article I had wanted to write. This part of the interview went well – very well.

The current affairs test was just as difficult as ever. I may as well not have bothered to read the newspapers. However, I answered the questions relating to news values very well. The people who had quizzed me said, "You'll receive the result of our meeting after Easter." I didn't think it could have been possible, but it was. They had recorded the interview. I heard a piece about post offices on *The Morning News* the following day. At the same time, my hand itched. They were telling me that the people who had examined me had recorded it. I couldn't believe it!

That gap needed to be filled again. I contacted Gerald, who said, "I'll treat your reading confidentially."

He said that he would, but he didn't. He seemed to think that I would get the place at WMU. I had already done parts of the course along the way, so it shouldn't be a problem. However, he claimed that I was too focused on wanting to go to university. I reminded him that I had applied for several jobs and hadn't got any of them. He said, "Some vacancies will be coming up later on in the year, and you should apply for the positions." He seemed to think that I was in with a good chance, so long as the applications fell into the right hands.

When I voiced my concern about somebody blocking the play, he didn't like it. He wanted to gloss over the matter. He knew as well as I did that someone had obstructed the play and that the stopping was terrible. He didn't like it when I reminded him about the letter that I'd received from WMU either.

The outcome of the reading was that a few days later, I heard part of an interview with a woman who had spoken to Robert Mugabe. When I had applied to IBN for the traineeship, I had said that I wanted to interview Robert Mugabe. Coincidence?

I dreamed that I saw the woman in the window again - one of the female presenters from *The Morning News*. Two days later, a letter came from Strepton University, saying, "Your application has not been successful."

Frances and I went shopping because I was looking for a new skirt. As always, I was talking about the experience I was going through. It was all that I talked about. In my view, this was a sign of unhappiness. She commented on the fact that I couldn't get on to courses and hinted that I wouldn't be going anywhere. What did she know? Who had she been talking to? Then she said, "WMU gave you an interview for the sake of it. It was about ticking boxes." Would they do that? If so, why? I had asked WMU if it would be all right to reapply. If it wasn't, why had not WMU said so at the time, instead of putting me through an interview they knew wouldn't get me anywhere?

On our way home, we stopped off at Norma's house. She was planning to alter it. I didn't think anything of it at the time, but when I spoke to her a couple of days later, she was pretty nasty.

Everything she said had a ring of truth about it, but it was reversed. She said, "You're flattering yourself in thinking that BNUK have purloined your work." Having your work stolen was hardly a compliment. If I had been asked, that would have been praise

– indeed. She went on to say, "You want to blame other people for your failures." But wasn't it true? I was ineffective because people were meddling? Finally, she said, "You're always the victim." Of course, I was the dupe, but what could I do about it? I couldn't go around harming people because violence was my only solution for dealing with bullying. That would be the only thing persecutors would understand.

According to Toby, on the other hand, "They're treating you in the way they are – disrespectfully – because the presenters know they will get away with it. You can't control them, so they can do what they like." Cowards.

I realised what Norma had said, sprang from a disappointment. But what had happened? In view of the fact that her anger had been aimed at me, it was clear I was at fault. Why? What had I done or not done? It never occurred to my sisters that I didn't know what they knew. Therefore, to lash out at me in this way was foolish.

Later in the week, when I went to the hairdresser with Frances, the subject wasn't mentioned. How could I raise it again after the claims she had made on Monday and what Norma had said a couple of days afterwards? My sisters were conspiring against me behind my back. Why? Was there something in it for them?

April 2008

On *The Morning News,* Kiss of Death was talking to the Information Commissioner about obtaining other people's work. If the work wasn't being sought for journalistic purposes, and the author hadn't granted permission, it was theft. I couldn't believe what I was hearing. I interpreted the broadcast as an admission of guilt – my work had been stolen all those years ago. After all, that's how this business had begun. I had heard an item that I believed stemmed from a story that I had written.

I had to respond; I couldn't leave this as it was. I would have to be careful about what I said. I wrote down a message, but I didn't like it.

It wasn't until the end of the week, when I came up with something I could send, and despatch it I did. In the meantime, I had an intriguing conversation with Toby. According to him, "BNUK will deny everything you allege because you've got no proof." Once again, he seemed to be talking as though he was on their side.

Three weeks had elapsed since I had attended the interview at WMU, and I still hadn't heard whether I was successful or not. Judging by what Frances had said, I wasn't going to get the place, but I needed to hear it from WMU themselves. I sent an email to Linda Hunt asking her if she could let me know the outcome. I felt a sensation after transmitting it. Maybe she wasn't going to send a response like she had done when I had first applied.

At the end of the week, I received a letter informing me that I had not been allocated a place on the course and that it would be the last time I would have the opportunity to apply. It was clear that somebody had written a response based on the recording of the interview. I thought Kiss of Death had written it. The letter filled me with disgust, but dreadfulness was what I had come to expect from these people.

I told Frances, "WMU didn't give me a place." She sympathised with me, and then we went on to have a most fascinating conversation. She implied that what was going on was about work and accused me of not wanting to do any. She brought up an instance from the past when she had put me in touch with somebody who wasn't in a position to offer a job, but whom I had not contacted. If the contact hadn't been about employment, why mention it?

If what was happening now was about work, why didn't somebody say so when I had written to BNUK in the autumn? Why had

The Unfulfilled Promise

Gerald never talked about there being a job out there for me? This was something he would have seen. I was paying him enough. Why tell me about forthcoming vacancies if there was a position for me now? Who could I ask? And what could I do to test the veracity of Frances' allegation? But the bigger question was this: could I work with people who were prepared to treat me in this way?

We got on to talking about the creative writing course that I'd studied. It was clear that Anna said something about me. The problem with Anna was that she was only interested in keeping us on as students. She was always pestering us about staying on to do the next level of her course. I was concerned about how I would pay for it and about the way she was treating me. She was nasty. She used to hold on to my work, and she made snide comments about me. I complained about her, but she took no notice. I had no option other than to leave, otherwise, I would have done her some harm. I wanted to know this: what was said about me? And was it really the case that BNUK was carrying out a vendetta against me on her behalf?

I went to see Raymond again. He didn't give me a reading this time. He just told me what to do. He said, "You ought to contact a literary agent about your play." I knew I had bought that writing manual for a reason. I asked him about being betrayed. He seemed to think that it wouldn't happen again. He insinuated that that was over. I went home bouncing with joy – cursing myself for not having thought about the idea of getting in touch with a literary agent.

Twenty-four hours later, I was at Perfect Matches, where one of the women read the list of agents responsible for theatre plays. There weren't very many of them, so she let me have all of the names and addresses listed.

Back at home, I composed a letter of introduction. The second agent I contacted sent me an email, saying, "Send us your play." Fantastic! It had worked.

May 2008

When I mentioned the idea of sending the play to a literary agent to Frances, she seemed to know about it. Had the idea really come from Raymond? Or had somebody from BNUK suggested that I should contact a literary agent?

BNUK gave me permission to write a letter of complaint. My grievances would cover a period of five years. It wasn't going to be an easy letter to write. In fact, it took ages. After writing and rewriting, I posted it. I had welcomed the opportunity to have had my say, and hoped that I would have no more trouble.

During that week, I had two dreams which were disturbing. In one of them, I saw Kiss of Death. Immediately, I associated him with blocking something. Around about this time, I was planning to resubmit an application to Trentford University. Either Trentford University notified BNUK that I had contacted them or my reader told them of my intention to reapply. In the other, my play was being brushed aside. Something had happened to it. Somebody had hindered it. The dream unsettled me so much that I went to see Shaun. He came to the same conclusion about the dream as I had done, but his reading indicated otherwise. The reading did not assuage me.

In the meantime, I was preparing my application to Trentford University. I decided to get a careers officer to look at it, so I went to the university.

It felt strange being back after all this time. The university seemed to be bigger than I could recollect. Although I had an idea where the careers centre was, the building appeared to have grown and was much more difficult to get around than I could remember. I was so grateful for the help I received.

I showed my application to the careers officer, who said, "It's good." However, she drew my attention to a couple of things I could mention. As I travelled back home, I thought about the experience I had gone through at university.

I had been a hard-working, quiet student. I spent most of my time studying. To help me, I found a fantastic team of readers. They read very well. They were a mixture of English students and foreign. All of them observed my only rule: if you can't come for whatever reason, let me know.

In the place where I lived, there was a bar, and I used to frequent it. It was nice and handy. Through staying where I did, I got to know a few of the students. This turned out to be good. In spite of the number of students on the course I was doing, I only got to know a few of them. I studied English with Philosophy. I liked the Philosophy more than I thought I would. There were times when I thought I should have majored in that instead of English.

Flicking through the newspaper one day, my reader and I came across a job I could apply for with IBN. It was a traineeship for a researcher. It looked good. The only problem was, despite being on the Internet for so long, we were never able to write anything on it. This meant I would have to get Perfect Matches to help me with the process of registering. It was either my reader or Perfect Matches who betrayed me over this. I will never understand how these people could allow themselves to be manipulated. To your face, they were your friends, but behind your back... This was an aspect of dependency that I was beginning to loathe.

I received a response to my letter of complaint. I went into Birmingham to read it, using the reading machine at the library. When I had finished reading it, I wondered for a fleeting moment whether I was mad. Then it occurred to me that BNUK would never admit to anything I had alleged because that's what these organisations do.

Also, whatever it was they were trying to do – and they were trying to do something – hadn't worked.

A reply came from Trentford University. As her opening gambit, the woman who phoned me wanted to know why I hadn't applied to WMU. I told her that I had, but the university turned me down. Then she asked me why had I changed my mind. She seemed to be under the impression that we had talked about doing a production course. I told her that I had applied for one, and the university concerned rejected me. Then she went on to say, "I don't think you can do the course because you're blind. How would you cope at a demonstration," she wanted to know. Then, according to her, "Your age is against you." She thought there was a more suitable course I could do. She said, "I'll let you know," and she did.

The course she recommended was up north in Sunderland, but I didn't like it. The only production course that I had seen and liked was in London, which would have been a privilege to attend.

Later, she despatched an email saying, "Strepton University have got experience in dealing with students with a visual impairment."

Knowing this, I spoke to Gerald, once I had secured an assurance that he would keep the reading confidential.

I lied to him because I didn't mention the conversation I'd had with Trentford University. Nevertheless, he seemed to think that I would get on to this course. If not, he indicated that something would turn up because, in the last resort, I would have the opportunity to submit a piece again that I had worked on previously.

With regard to sending the play to a literary agent, Gerald appeared to think that I would hear something. The agent would want to see me. He seemed to imply that I ought to be ashamed in some way. Why should I? If the agent was going to help me, I would be more than delighted to meet him. Then he went on to criticise what I'd written when submitting the play. He said, "You didn't sell yourself enough." Whatever I had written had been sufficient for the agent to ask me to send my play. But how did Gerald know what I had written? This was something he couldn't possibly have known unless he had been told. Had he been told? If so, by whom?

In a sense, this reminded me of the references. Linda Hunt had said that it was all right to use the testimonials that I had, yet BNUK, who had no right to see the applications nor what I had written when submitting my play, was saying otherwise. The station was telling people who knew their job how to do it. They were just throwing their weight around.

At around half past five on Monday 19th May, somebody blocked the application to Trentford University. Whoever had done it, had done it on behalf of The Child. When I checked my emails an hour later, there was one from the university, saying, "Your application has not been successful."

Aware of what they had done, the presenter and guests on *The Morning News* went on to discuss social mobility – why wasn't it happening and so on. Debates like this always struck me as perverse.

When I spoke to Norma the following day, she urged me to write a book. She said, "The presenters involved in this affair don't want you around." I had started to write a memoir, but I had abandoned it because I thought it would be libelous. Given that I had received a letter from BNUK denying everything that I had claimed, this meant I could write it. With regard to the current situation, Norma was giving me a warning.

On *The Morning News* two days later, I caught reference to Sunderland, the university which the woman from Trentford University had recommended, and to IBN, where I was applying for a place on their training scheme. I should have realised that these references signified something.

I had decided to go into Birmingham to read a document using the reading machine. As I travelled on the bus, I had the most excruciating ear-burning sensation. It was negative; someone was cursing me. Why? What had I not done?

When I got home, I understood the importance of what Norma had said two days ago. The literary agent had returned my play. It was clear that Gerald had lied. He had known when I called him on Friday that the play had been blocked — that was how he knew what I had written. This was nothing more than a piece of wickedness. He wasn't working for me. He was working for them. I had asked him to treat the reading confidentially. I emailed him. He sent back some nonsense saying, "I'm helping you to the best of my ability." He was betraying me more like. He must have known what would happen if they knew that I had submitted my play. They were merciless. Our relationship would have to end. He clearly didn't value it, all because of the Child. Although I was paying him, I was trash.

When I spoke to Frances two days later, I let her know in no uncertain terms what I thought. Her response was to go and tell The Child.

I was still working on the application for a place on the training scheme with IBN when my reader told me, "There are some vacancies at BNUK." Gerald had said that some jobs would come up. In fact, I had forgotten about his prediction. However, he had pointed out that I would only get a job if the application fell into the right hands.

June 2008

My reader helped me to look at the information about the vacancies at BNUK, and eventually, we downloaded it. Then I worked on it.

The Unfulfilled Promise

By now, we had sorted out the problem with writing on the Internet. It was a matter of clicking some options on the speech software.

For this application, applicants had to write an essay answer. I wrote my essay on diverse communities. I must confess, diverse communities weren't something I readily thought about. Within the space allocated, I wrote about these communities and the only group I could not mention was the elderly. This was because I would have exceeded the character limit.

One of the problems I had in completing this application form was working in characters. I had never done this before. In fact, as a consequence of not knowing how many characters equalled a page, I had difficulty knowing how much to write. I wrote as much as I could within the character space allowed. It struck me that I had done the best that I could.

When it came to filling in the form, it looked as though I could have written more than I had, or at least, I could have better organised what I had written.

When I woke up the following morning, I realised I could have done things differently. I was in a panic. Was there anything I could do about it? Feeling somehow that I hadn't understood the characters idea, I mentioned it to Raymond. He said, "You could say something to BNUK. Evidently, the information was not clear." I did this, but after talking to a person at human resources, I felt I had done everything right. It was just a matter of waiting.

On *The Morning News* the following day, I heard an interview with a group of old people who wanted to die even though they were in good health. The elderly was the only group I had not mentioned in my essay. Was this aimed at me? Was Kiss of Death expecting me to comment on this? I shrank from the idea. It was repulsive. So far as I was concerned, he was telling me that he had scuppered my application. Later, I dreamed it was Raymond who had enabled him to do so. What a spiteful man.

At the end of that week, I heard a piece on *The Morning News* that reminded me of something I'd written. The presenter and guests were talking about a soap opera. I remembered that I had heard about a job as a writer for one of the soap operas. I applied for it with a passion, and I very much enjoyed working on the application. Sadly, I did not get the job. I hadn't even been invited to attend an interview. Several days later, I sent in a note, but I received no reply.

Meanwhile, I submitted the application for IBN, but Kiss of Death had blocked this too. I caught something about teaching mathematics. Many years ago, I had worked as a volunteer, teaching basic numeracy.

I went to see Hazel. I was really looking for something, but somehow, I couldn't find it. Her reading left a lot to be desired. I suspected it from the start. She said, "You ought to go to the newspapers about the fact that you've been rejected from so many universities." She saw it as racism. I had never thought of going to a newspaper about my story.

Sometimes going to the press can make things worse. She went on to talk about my sister and her children and how they held me in high regard. She mentioned my neighbours too. I thought this was odd. She alluded to a lot of other things that didn't make sense.

Hazel referred to The Child. Once again, he was criticised, and I was warned to steer clear of him. Why was this? Why was it that all the clairvoyants I had spoken to had nothing good to say about the Child? I found this concerning.

Out of the blue, she mentioned Kiss of Death. She asked me if I knew anyone by the name of -. I told her that the only — I knew was the one obstructing my progress. It sounded as though she was saying, "He wants to help you," but it transpired that she was advising me not to have anything more to do with him either.

This idea of being supported by somebody who had systematically undermined everything I was trying to do was nonsense.

I came to the conclusion that somebody had spoken to Hazel. Looking back, on the night before I had gone to see her, my ears had burned like a doorbell ringing. I hadn't been able to understand why, but it was clear they rang in anticipation of what Hazel would say in the reading. Why were these presenters meddling with the clairvoyants when they didn't know what my beliefs were with regard to them?

As I left Hazel's house, I asked her a question, "Am I missing out on an opportunity? Did BNUK have a job to offer, or was it just a game?" She said, "You haven't missed out on anything."

What had happened? Had something passed me by? When I spoke to Norma again, the conversation quickly turned sour. She said, "Clairvoyants have given hope that has come to nothing."

What was she talking about? I said, "They haven't given hope." I knew only too well that what they said could come true, as well as it might not. What was important about Norma's tone was it was clear she was more dependent on the readings than I was. But how would she have known what they had said? I had never discussed this with her. Her manner shocked me. Evidently, she had not realised that what was going on had disappointed me too.

Norma accused me of putting myself on the centre stage when I went to see these clairvoyants. Of course, she was telling me that the clairvoyants were recording my readings and letting certain people listen to them, just as I had suspected. But why? I wasn't a terrorist. I was nowhere near approaching such a thing, yet...I remembered something.

One evening, Norma had phoned me simply to ask for my nephew's number. This was unusual because she could so easily have got it from Martha. After all, Martha and Norma got on very well together. Had she known about the forthcoming reading that I was going to have with Hazel?

At the time of the reading, Hazel's references to my sister and to her children, and to the fact that I did not get on so well with one of my neighbours, surprised me. It couldn't be possible, and yet...

I phoned Martha. She couldn't remember when Norma had phoned about her son's number, but she went on to say how she thought I deserved a chance. She said, "You're at the top of my wishlist - for an opportunity." I could hardly hold back my tears.

She pointed out that there are people out there who won't do a thing. Then she made a coment which was a real memory jerker, "You've only failed when you've given up." This was something our father used to say. Our father – what would our father have made of the situation I was in?

He would have been appalled that my efforts weren't being rewarded in some way. When I had gone to work, he always complained that it wasn't worthwhile. I was working for nothing. Then one day, my employers gave me a full-time job, but working full-time was no better than working part-time.

The work I did was boring – typing the same letter over and over again. The monotony was broken when my employer asked me to take minutes at council meetings. When it came to the upgrading of the typewriter I used, there was a row.

One of the people I worked for thought I should have a modern typewriter, but my supervisor thought differently. In the end, the head of the department gave me a new typewriter, which made my supervisor realise she should have given me one in the first place. She oversaw the arrival of new typewriters for all of the other women a long time ago, but this wasn't the only respect in which my employer treated me differently.

The supervisor encouraged the girls to undertake further studies if they wanted to, but I was never offered such an opportunity. Who would have listened to me? The problem with the supervisor was that the only person she liked was herself. Her predecessor was stern but fair. I will never forget the day when she came to work crying like a baby because her partner left her.

The supervisor was probably in her mid-forties at the time, and her partner was about nine years younger than she was. They definitely saw themselves as going up in the world because they bought a bungalow in the countryside. What the supervisor failed to realise was that the lifestyle she was living wasn't what her partner wanted.

One day, she faced up to the fact that she was too old for him. He wanted children, and he found himself a partner who could give them to him. As blunt as that may sound, it was evidently the truth as her partner saw it. It was embarrassing seeing an older woman cry in the way she had done.

Having said that about my father, the situation I was in was partly due to him.

When my parents had purchased the house I live in, my name was included on the deeds. In the event of my parents' death, I would have inherited the house outright. However, one day, my father made up his mind that he didn't want me to inherit the entire house. This was because, if I got married, he didn't like the idea of my husband getting all of the money he earned. He decided the property should be split. After much argument and very much under duress, I signed a "tenants in common agreement." This meant that I owned half of the house, and the rest belonged to my sisters. At the time, I saw it as a debt and worried enormously about it. I had done what my parents wanted, and my sisters knew it. However, from time to time, I was made to feel uneasy by people who were better placed than I was.

The following day, Frances and I went for a stroll on the hills. While we were walking, she dropped the biggest hint yet about what was happening, "BNUK have been trying to force you to make contact with The Child." She didn't explain why. She just said, "They've put you through two years of misery because of him." Ironically, he was the very first person who I had approached in this affair, but that didn't matter now. When I went on to help myself, he got in the way. Worse still, he sat back while Kiss of Death took away most of the opportunities I had created for myself. Then he and Kiss of Death got into bed with my family, almost turning them against me. How I resented him. The idea of speaking to him – and I believe that talking to him was what they wanted - repulsed me.

Was it wise to try to force somebody to go on to a phone-in, knowing that doing so was regarded as a voluntary act of participation? The idea was grotesque. What sort of a person saw himself as so great that he believed somebody should be coerced into speaking to him? What would have been wrong with getting somebody to say something to me? At least that way everybody would have been sure that I understood what was going on. As it was, I was left guessing and spelling – trying to work out what was happening. The question I would like an answer to is this: was there really a position?

Frances hinted as much, but was it really the role of presenters to hand out jobs? And would BNUK have sanctioned work being offered in this way? I doubted it very much.

I believed Gerald was advising me on behalf of someone at BNUK who was responsible, but Kiss of Death and The Child didn't like it. When I put this idea to Frances, she didn't deny it.

Throughout this period, I always wanted to write a letter to find out what was going on and where I stood, but I never did so because I feared that nobody would reply, as was the case last time.

It was clear that Norma felt at liberty to get in touch with BNUK and, perhaps, with Kiss of Death in particular. I had told her that the book I was writing was going to take the form of a diary. Before I knew it, *The Morning News* broadcast an item that was written in a diary form. It was an account of somebody's experience in Zimbabwe. To be honest, when I heard it, I thought nothing of it. It was when I caught a journal entry on a different programme that I realised that Norma must have said something.

Was it really wise to have encouraged my sisters to believe that if they supplied information about me, and I spoke out, they would be rewarded for it? That was the arrangement, wasn't it? The only problem was, whenever I heard anything that sounded familiar, I only recognised the source and experienced an enormous sense of hurt at being betrayed.

July 2008

I didn't get the job I had applied for. BNUK didn't give a reason in the email they sent to me. The following day, Kiss of Death sounded highly amused by something. According to Frances, "You didn't get the job because it's in London." There was always an excuse for not getting these things, but how would she have known why?

A woman was looking back at how the authorities had treated her daughter's death. She didn't think they had handled it very well, "If only..." she said, "things would have been different." I whole-heartedly sympathised with this woman to the extent that I sent in a comment (which nobody answered) saying as much. My point being that, if only somebody had done what he should have done, things could have been very different for me too. But they weren't.

The Child should have helped me, but he didn't want to fulfil the promise. He went on to do something which pleased himself: deceive others into believing that I had to contact him. He did this because he was sure I could not prove that it was he who should have contacted me. As a result of this tactic, I was the one who suffered because nobody else was allowed to support me.

If the arrangement had been changed, something ought to have been said or communicated, but nothing was said or conveyed. If they were depending on my psychic ability, that had already been used and abused; and I wasn't going to allow it to occur again. If there was anything to know, I wanted to be told, and I had said as much in the consultation I had had with the counsellor in 2006. Evidently, this was a viewpoint that nobody wanted to hear. I was only too aware that, as a listener, I could take part in discussions and debates as and when I liked, but not as a result of psychological bullying.

I accepted long ago that what had happened or what had not happened in 2003 had gone wrong. For some unknown reason, The Child could not accept this. My reaction was to try to help myself, but I had to be stopped and prevented. This then was how the spy base had come into being.

Everybody who knew me had to spy, betray me, and/or report on what I said, where I went, and what I did. I believe that, in pursuing this, The Child was trying to recreate the past. In his bid to do so, my life's experiences had to be ransacked.

Together with his colleagues, he had found out as much about my life as he possibly could with a view to turning the information into a package. When this was broadcast, it would force me to respond. This being the case, nothing ever needed to be said, because in their minds, this strategy would work. After all, it was what had taken place in 2003, but was it? What had I reacted to in 2003? By virtue of the fact that they had no idea of what it was that I had responded to, it was very unwise to try to revive the experience.

The Unfulfilled Promise

But why was it so imperative to want to reproduce the past? It was one of two things: one, he was guilty for not acting when he should have done. Or two, he wanted to prove that I could not succeed without him, and he wanted to receive the praise and the plaudits he would have gained if this had been successful in 2003. I had no doubt in my mind that if this had worked when it should have, it would have been the stuff of newspaper headlines both at home and abroad. But it hadn't worked because The Child had been unable to act.

This was a promise which should have been fulfilled at the time it was made, not when it suited The Child to do so.

Afterwards

In August 2008, I received two offers to study the graduate diploma in law, but due to circumstances beyond my control I was unable to take up either of these offers.

In October 2008, I received an unexpected postcard from Dramatique. On it was information about a forthcoming screenwriting course for disabled people. However, when I inquired about the course, the providers said that it had been postponed due to a lack of numbers.

Five months later, on a bright but chilly morning, I set out to attend the first of four sessions on writing for the screen. At the end of this great course, my screenplay was selected to be read at a festival of disabled filmmakers.

In December 2008, my brother told me that the stories that triggered the events narrated in this book had been stolen from the organisation with whom I was studying a creative writing course. My brother was anxious to point out that BNUK itself had not purloined the stories, but an individual within that organisation had done so.

Much later, I found out why I had not got on to any of the courses that I had applied for. The woman in the window— a female presenter from *The Morning News* – lied about my qualifications. It was this lie that Kiss of Death had used to prevent me from getting on to the courses I had applied for and for not getting some of those jobs.

Whenever I hear "Coming up in the next hour," or "Coming up later," I am reminded of how I used to introduce the content of my programmes because these were the phrases I always used.

www.ingramcontent.com/pod-product-compliance
Lightning Source LLC
LaVergne TN
LVHW021237080526
838199LV00088B/4565